MUMBAI

Mumbai

A city of dreams

edited by

MALVIKA SINGH

ACADEMIC FOUNDATION
NEW DELHI

www.academicfoundation.com

First published in 2011
by

ACADEMIC FOUNDATION
4772-73 / 23 Bharat Ram Road, (23 Ansari Road),
Darya Ganj, New Delhi - 110 002 (India).
Phones : 23245001 / 02 / 03 / 04.
Fax : +91-11-23245005.
E-mail : books@academicfoundation.com
www.academicfoundation.com

Cataloging in Publication Data--DK
Courtesy: D.K. Agencies (P) Ltd. <docinfo@dkagencies.com>

Mumbai : a city of dreams / edited by Malvika Singh.
p. cm.
ISBN 13: 9788171888870
ISBN 10: 8171888879

1. Bombay (India)--History. 2. Bombay (India)--Social life and customs. I. Singh, Malvika.

DDC 954.792 22

Typeset by Italics India, New Delhi.
Printed and bound in India.

For

SHASHI KAPOOR

Contents

Introduction

MALVIKA SINGH

The journal SEMINAR turned fifty in the year 2009. At that time we decided to bring out themed 'compendiums' from the vast treasure of material that the monthly had published over the five and more, decades. As part of that ongoing project, Academic Foundation have reproduced six special issues of SEMINAR, as a set of individual books, that celebrate the historic and famed cities of Delhi; Bombay, now Mumbai; Calcutta, now Kolkata; Madras, now Chennai; Hyderabad and Lucknow. We are delighted that this work will be accessible to a wider audience of Indians as well as visitors to India, who would want to share and experience the many special, personal and individual insights into the life and times of these cities, based on memories, on hitherto unspoken behind-the-scenes stories, some full of joy and others that lament the change, all of which are woven together in an extraordinary tapestry.

My gratitude to Rituraj and Sanu Kapila for having recognised the merit of these carefully crafted mini compendiums, and for reproducing them with much care. My thanks to all the writers who participated in the issues of SEMINAR, making them lively, unusual and substantive. To my colleagues at SEMINAR, my sincere thanks for supporting the many SEMINAR related 'ventures' like this one!

A city of dreams

HARSH SETHI

THE city of hope, of dreams, of opportunity – this is how Bombay appears to the migrant. All large cities have their repertoire of rags to riches stories. But it is only Bombay that has immortalized the metamorphosis in numerous cinematic representations. Just think of Amitabh Bachchan in *Deewar*.

For close to two centuries, in particular after the setting up of the textile mills and then the railways, Bombay remained the favoured destination of anyone who wanted to seek his fortune. In the early days, land was not in short supply. Equally, the industrialists, unlike in many other urban centres actually set up infrastructure for the growing industrial workforce, the *chawls* of Dadar and Parel. The migrants both created wealth and enriched the culture of the city. No surprise that at the time of independence, Bombay was our most vibrant, multicultural and welcoming city. It was also republican, the generation of wealth modulated by a respect for labour, helped no doubt by the communist control of the textile unions. In short, it created a work ethic.

Unlike many of our traditional cities which grew around religious complexes and princely courts or were colonial creations which thrived on the exercise of power, Bombay has remained quintessentially capitalist – modern, forward looking, intent on getting the work done. Of course, the wealthy enjoyed a lifestyle of privilege, even ostentation. But again, unlike most other centres in the country, they evolved a culture of giving back to the city, the lead being taken by the Parsi elite. The other rich – the Gujarati and Marwari businessmen, the Khoja and Bohra Muslims, even the professional elite – did not lag behind. The many institutions in the city – from hospital and colleges to art galleries and museums – are testimony to both a civic consciousness and pride.

It is unclear what role geography played in the evolution of the city. The port was the connection to worlds afar, the railway network to the hinterland. Connecting the island to the mainland led to a linear growth, the first to be ably serviced by a suburban system. Constraints of space forced people to build upwards, giving the country its first skyscrapers. Managing densities has rarely been an Indian skill, but most impartial observers will agree that Bombay was for long our best managed urban space. It worked, in fact had to, for there is little margin for error.

Modern business requires both discipline and order, qualities that Bombay has demonstrated in abundance. Unlike Delhi and Calcutta, the two other early megalopolises, the city spends least time in peripheral politicking. Fewer people are interested in those who wield political power, the pride of place being reserved for businessmen and increasingly now film stars. Not that the city was ever apolitical. Prior to Delhi hegemonizing all political space, the locus of nationalist, anti-colonial activity was Bombay and Calcutta.

It is not clear when this model of urban living started unravelling. May be it started with the Samyukta Maharashtra movement for creating Maharashtra as a separate state with Bombay as its capital. Possibly there was a reaction to a consistent under representation of the local Marathi speaking populace in the power structure. What is undeniable was also the reaction to the glaring inequalities of wealth and income.

With over half the city's population living in slums and on pavements, or squeezed out into the far peripheries, the climate was ripe for a variety of populist and revanchist movements. Led by Bal Thackeray, cartoonist and demagogue, the Shiv Sena sought to buttress Marathi pride and renegotiate the placement of the 'natives' in the power structure by first targeting the Tamils. Now, of course, the favourite whipping boys are provided by the Muslim community. The party first secured control of the municipal corporation, subsequently expanding to seize the reins of power of the state.

It is not as if the 'decline' of Bombay, now Mumbai – the growth of crime and resultant insecurity; an increasing ghettoization of different communities, what sociologist Narendra Panjwani once described as a city of trenches; the erosion of its once-famed tolerance and welcoming spirit – can be traced only or primarily to the rise of the Shiv Sena. Many other factors – demographic, economic and political – have come together to transform this metropolis, possibly for the worse.

Take first, the size and the rapidity with which the city has grown in the last five decades, straining its infrastructure beyond endurance. Crime there always was. But the transformation of petty smuggling occasioned by a regime of shortages, helped by the fact of Bombay as a port, to organized mafia gangs into construction and extortion is a more recent phenomenon. But, what irretrievably changed the city was the demise of the textile industry. Why this happened – policy, lack of investment in technology, labour militancy particularly under the late Datta Samant – is debatable. Just read the brilliant study by Darryl D'Monte. What is clearer are the consequences – large number of workers forced into the informal sector adding to the foot-soldiers in crime and the release of prime urban space for speculation. More than anything else, the politics of the city is now fuelled by fights over control of the erstwhile mill land.

How Bombay has changed. For a start it is no longer an industrial city; wealth generation is now accounted for by finance, trade, services and entertainment. This requires a transformed infrastructure and a different, white collar workforce. In all likelihood this process has further marginalized the 'natives', less equipped to break into the high value, high returns sectors. There is also the sediment of decades of communal and sectarian politics. No longer is this a city where citizens can freely walk around late at night and since the law rarely favours the weak, security is sought by relying on and living with one's own.

There is also the less noticed relationship with the hinterland. The city may well generate over half the state domestic product and taxes. It also guzzles up a disproportionate share of public goods – particularly water and electricity. With little symbiosis and complimentarity between the metropole and the countryside, anger with the city and its residents has grown. They, including those in ill-serviced slums or pavements, are seen by the rest as privileged. Consequently, subsidies by the state to maintain and upgrade the infrastructure necessary for a large megalopolis have shrunk, generating further pressure. It is symptomatic that the municipal corporation of Mumbai, once the richest in the country, has for the last decade been in the red.

Accompanying this is the flight of the elite, at least metaphorically. They now remain cocooned in their enclaves – from the gracious mansions of Malabar Hill to the aesthetic monstrosities of a Hafeez Contractor, cut off from the ordinary citizenry. Surely it is difficult to deny that unlike the colonial times, the rich have created few institutions of consequence in the last five decades.

Nevertheless, the city retains a vibrancy. Be it the famed *dabbawallas* whose operations are now studied in all leading business schools or the numerous civic groups and associations – the city continues to fight back. To retain and nurture its legacy, to maintain its openness to outsiders and to migrants. It is this that has helped it survive and grow and it is this which unthinking proposals of introducing a city permit and throwing out 'outsiders' threatens. This volume is an ode to our first city, a city of dreams.

Decline of a great city

GERSON DA CUNHA

Bombay Wallahs*

Nowhere is ever home but this may be the town of least effort for me.
Here the idiom is known. Saris curdle over haunch like nowhere else.
Lust kindles in the silver dark at the starlet's launch and hot from home
tin lunches clatter out under a Gothic arch.

Seven islands soaked up the sea to leave land for an infanta's dowry.
For two hundred years and more the tides have swept the world ashore
The thought air teems. A bow of water curves from slum to dream to
loose an arrow's flight. On the walls our blood spills black and white.

IN the fifties, into the sixties, they all came back to Bombay, those who went abroad to study and train. Many voyaged across the seas to live here. They do not return any more, or come from other lands to stay. The young ones used to come home for the good living to be had here, but also for a commodity once as plentiful as the jobs:

* 'Bombay Wallahs' has been taken from *So Far: a collection of poems* by Gerson da Cunha.

the hope. Where is either to be found these days, even in respectable fragments, never mind the abundance of yore?

I remember my city 50 years ago for the daily washing of its streets with chlorinated water. I remember my home in Mazgaon, one of the original hills of Bombay. Each evening, you could hear the animals at feeding time in Victoria Gardens Zoo, two miles away as the lion roars. Not any more. You hear only the bellow and snarl of traffic. We had our own gardens, as a matter of fact, with a great peepul, a raintree and an acacia among a dozen fruit-bearing trees. It was a welcoming, hopeful city in a newly free nation.

Clean streets, lions at dinner audible miles away and rambling gardens in fairly crowded localities make a point about the city. There was an amplitude about it, even in the *wadis* of Girgaum and neighbourhoods of Parel. They were busy and crowded certainly, but the people filled spaces that were planned for them, designed for those numbers: in BDD chawls, built by the venerable Bombay Development Department, and the 'quarters' for mill, city and railway employees. Citizens lived and worked to an orderly city plan, paying sensible prices for space, without land grab and vote bank politics, as at present.

Did we but know it then, these were all marks of a great city. The economics of Bombay has a history and a strong hand in its distinctive make up. Halfway through the 19th century, a new era had dawned for this huddle of fishermen's rocks around a wonderful harbour. The Suez Canal spelled great days for Bombay as a port and allied businesses, as did the American Civil War for Indian cotton, which of course needed the port to go out to the world. After the Indian uprising of 1857 against Britain, the new imperial power chose to make an imperial statement here, as its main public buildings testify – the High Court, University, Secretariat, Municipality, the Town Hall and later the Prince of Wales Museum, then the great railway buildings rivalling King's Cross and St. Pancras in London.

By the turn of the last century, Bombay was a world city by the sea to which international trade and commerce came; witness the

Sassoon and Kadourie families taking refuge from Baghdad among countless others who came as merchants and professionals.

Wealth of a certain kind attracts the arts – public statuary and private collections of painting and sculpture – as well as the graces of secondary businesses which catch the spirit of the times, as in the proud department stores of Hornby Road and Mahatma Gandhi Road, Evans and Fraser, Whiteways Laidlaw (now the Khadi and Village Industries Emporium filled with crores worth of non-saleable goods and unsalesworthy employees), the Army and Navy Stores, even such frivolities as Fucile the hairdressers and the merry Italian cafes and confectioneries – Cornaglia, Mongini, Comba, Bertorellis and, a bit later, Bombellis.

People with the option to live and move elsewhere seemed to prefer Bombay just after the war. May be independence does something for a nation, like spring for a woman's skin and a young man's fancy. The world was looking hard at India – and at Bombay, its best known international address. It was not at all a bad place to be.

There was an adequacy of recreational space. Housing was good, and good at various price levels, bungalows and apartment blocks. Water, sanitation and electric power supply were uniformly good. Bombay's buses and trams got you about quickly and cheaply, often over considerable distances on an island shaped like a hand extended in greeting. Streets, roads and traffic were easily negotiable. There was Marine Drive. Then, as now, the main transport lifelines were the two suburban railways, called at the time the BB&CI and GIP Railways, both of whom had world-beating hockey teams, I remember (the rest of the world not being great at the game) and when the two met it was an epic city encounter.

It is when the basics of life are routinely delivered, as they once were in Bombay, that a city's mind discovers itself. Hunger must be appeased daily before cuisine makes any sense. It happened here. The city attracted and held high quality people. Such talent can choose to go where it pleases. It chose Bombay substantially in the decade or so after independence. Its economics, quality of life and openness had much to do with the decisions. Mumbai no longer beckons that way. Even in colonial times, the city's governance was much more accountable to citizens than it is now.

The energy of a city is based as much on the toil of its workers as on its intellectual muscle and authority. Certainly, Bombay was partly a product of the surpluses generated by its workforce. But just now, I am concerned with its other vital forces. A fellow worker of mine who ended up heading India's scientific establishment once said, 'If we don't have our aristocracies, we can't have great thinking.' To continue in this vein of controversial thought, Goethe has said somewhere, 'A fig for your majorities! Wisdom never dwelt but with the few.' We must look at the minorities of that Bombay. It is they who caused the city to live up to the motto on its escutcheon, valid for a century and more, '*Urbs prima in Indis*' (First City of India).

In the late forties and all of the fifties, Bombay offered a roll call of enduring eminence. Homi Bhabha, polymath father of our atomic energy initiatives, and Vikram Sarabhai, early researcher into space and satellites, were city men honoured in the world science of their times. The Progressive Artists Group near Kala Ghoda, (an equestrian statue of Edward VII on Rampart Row) brought modern art to India. It was inspired by refugees in the city from Hitler's Europe, Walter Langhammer, who became Art Director of *The Times of India*, and Rudi von Leyden, who entered commercial life in Volkart's, then Voltas. The PAG men who mixed the first colours of modern art in India included M.F. Hussain and Ara, brilliant painter of still life whose nudes suddenly caused jaws to sag in the brand new Jehangir Art Gallery; Raza, later to make a notable mark in Paris where he lives now; though not a member of PAG, a painter was at work in Grindlays, a nearby bank, Krishen Khanna.

In the city's realms of industry and finance were the youthful J.R.D. Tata and Keshub Mahindra, to say nothing of G.D. Birla himself, the Wadias and Dalmias (in a remarkable coup, Ramkrishna bought *The Times of India*, which is like saying he picked up the British Empire while shopping one Friday). Shakila Bano Bhopali sang regularly to rapidly growing audiences on Lamington Road; Omkar Nath Thakur enraptured music lovers in *pandals* on Azad Maidan; Uday Shankar was unveiling totally new dance forms.

Bombay was the bastion in India of western classical music. Where else were there enough Goans to play second violin and the violas in an orchestra? This was the home of Mehli Mehta, father of Maestro Zubin and leader of the Bombay Symphony Orchestra. It was conducted by the Belgian Jules Craen who often featured his concert pianist wife, Olga. First Egidio Verga, then Colaba's very own George Lester brought the magic of the cello to the city. Walter Kaufman was here before returning to his native Vienna to help, then lead, the postwar development of the Vienna Philharmonic Society. It was Mehli Mehta and Verga who composed and executed the haunting time signal of All India Radio, a soaring violin heard over a cello drone pretending to be a tanpura.

Mulk Raj Anand worked with spitfire energy on new novels post-*Coolie,* essays and criticism in literature and art. Nissim Ezekiel, back from cheerless London in the mid- fifties, was finding his own and India's voice in English poetry. His contribution was already beginning to be significant, as much in his generous support of fellow-writers as in his own prolific work.

As the PAG did for modern art, Ebrahim Alkazi brought modern European theatre to India. Kuwaiti by parentage but Poona born and raised, Alkazi was introduced to theatre by the remarkable Sultan Padamsee in his Theatre Group, Bombay. Padamsee died at the age of 24. But by then he had upturned the city's life in theatre, poetry and painting. Alkazi snatched up the fallen standard of new theatre that Padamsee had raised. In the early sixties he went to New Delhi where, even if he did not actually found it, he set the high traditions and style of the National School of Drama as its Director. In Marathi theatre, P.L. Deshpande and Vijay Tendulkar were surprising audiences with anything but conventional work, to wit Deshpande's one-man '*Batatyachi chaal*' (Potato Chawl).

Watson's Hotel, Bombay is where the movies came in 1897, barely six months after the brothers Lumiere had presented their epoch-making *Cinematographie* in Paris. That's how high Bombay ranked worldwide for innovation and commercial value. It never left the vanguard of cinema. Today, it is the world's most active city in film production.

The fifties were the high point of the black-and-white masterpiece. Much influenced by Italian neo-realism, Raj Kapoor, Bimal Roy, Guru Dutt, Mehboob Khan and Navketan (Dev Anand) reigned when the lights went down in the nation's theatres. They functioned out of Bombay. Pre-eminently, it was the age, at least the coming of age, of Raj Kapoor.

His name links immediately with the magical Nargis, his co-star in *Barsaat* (1949) and *Awara* (1951). With the first, he also established his signature ensemble, composers Shankar and Jaikishen, lyricists Shailendra and Hazrat Jaipuri and singers Lata Mangeshkar and Mukesh. Like Barsaat, Awara was box office bonanza. B.D. Garga in his authoritative work *So Many Cinemas*, says of Awara: '...an astonishing, even ingenious mixture of melodrama, romance and a Ziegfield style dream sequence (it) seduced audiences (everywhere). In postwar, post-partition India, when the entire socio-political system was under strain and thousands of migrants poured into the cities, identification with Raj Kapoor's dispossessed, rootless Raju was plausible and easy.'

The kaleidoscope has many colours and shapes. But the details may fail to depict an essential and larger phenomenon going on in the city, the fusing of the city's disparate elements into its cosmopolitanism. High quality minds and spirits became greater because, like elements with unsatisfied valencies in an environment of constant collision, they combined to form valuable new compounds.

'It was all a bit like a continuous party,' says poet and writer Dom Moraes, 'Never planned. But it never stopped.' He was speaking about what went on in the home of his father, Frank Moraes, first Indian to be editor of *The Times of India*, war correspondent and a personality of many vivid hues. Dom remembers their flat in 'Green Fields' on the Oval at Churchgate. It was a scene of perpetual comings and goings of everybody from D.G. Tendulkar, the definitive Gandhi biographer, to Jawaharlal Nehru and British civil servants, down to a fleeing nationalist wanted by the police. This gentleman was tracked down one evening to the flat by a British police inspector. The cop left after a drink with the assembled revellers, among whom he had recognized his quarry. They shook hands. No arrest was made. Nobody cared to disentangle the linkages and forces responsible.

Such networks were numerous. Camellia Punjabi, lately of the Taj hotels, tells of friendships with Jayant Narlikar and Vikram Sarabhai. 'I asked Narlikar, much to my embarrassment when I thought about it later... I mean, there I was with this world famous cosmologist and I said, "Tell me do you believe in astrology?"' She recalls a conversation with Sarabhai as long as half a century ago. He said to her, 'One day, Camellia, we'll put satellites into space that will fill India with milk.' She is still mystified by the reference to Operation Flood. But he was right about the satellites.

Strangely, I became aware of religion, caste and community only as independence approached. It was impossible to ignore the demand for Pakistan and its rationale. In school, we knew each other by surnames and a surname, whether Crawford, Habib, Udwadia, Jain or Chatterjee was just that, a way of yelling out to someone across a playing field. The rest of the town was much the same, a melting pot of communities. I now know there was a consciousness of community. But the differences did not mean the separateness and threat that some elements pose to others today.

I graduated from St. Xavier's College. In my day, it was powered by some remarkable Jesuits and some no less distinguished non-clerics. The day after the first atomic bomb exploded over Hiroshima, Fr. R. Rafael, head of the Physics department, told us in a hastily convened lecture how the split atom delivers its colossal energies. This was not an unknown subject even then. But he went on to suggest how it might all have been put together, a much less trafficked aspect of the bang. It was rumoured that he knew in his pre-Jesuit days one of the men who worked on the Manhattan project in New Mexico.

Fr. F. Vion was a world class mathematician. Fr. H. Santapau was a botanist, good enough, despite being a foreigner and a priest, to be named the first head of the Botanical Survey of India. There was Fr. J. Duhr, a hard to situate individual who ranged in his lectures from Aristophanes and exploits of Hammurabi to the Napoleonic wars. He had a section all to himself in the college magazine entitled 'Duhr among the books.' Fr. H. Heras, of the Indian Historical Research Institute that he established in the college, is credited with having cracked the written code of Mohenjo Daro. Professors Kothari, C.D. Pinto, Theophilus Aguiar and Mhatre made waves that were not just citywide but went well beyond. The hot focus of effort was of course the students of these men in the century-old place at Dhobi Talao.

While this was true of St. Xavier's, other institutions were no laggards, Elphinstone and Grant Medical, the JJ School of Art and Architecture and the University Department of Chemical Technology. All this is meant to suggest the academic clime of the period. It was stimulating and nurturing, with a figure like Vithal Chandavarkar presiding over the affairs of the university as Vice Chancellor.

A great city's academics must obviously be doing the right thing at two levels, as faculty and as graduating students. They were pretty much all that they should have been in the fifties and early sixties. This did not fail to have an impact on the city's intellectual and professional life. I bring this up because of the depths to which this facet of city life has plummeted, where leaked question papers, marks scams, postponed examinations and results, admission irregularities amid centralized tests, worthless political appointments to headship of departments and ideologically tainted textbooks pass unnoticed as routine.

Today, Mumbai University is a degree factory, a necessary marshalling point for departures to foreign universities. Worst of all, the portents suggest yet tighter centralization, greater financial lacks and further deterioration in academic standards.

This is a world away from all that characterized a city of great talent and thrust, with many globally competitive advantages, as we might put it today. What went wrong?

In three little words, the city's politics.

They have turned a good thing into something that yields bad outcomes. Democracy is being used for competitive populism and to protect the corrupt and the malefactor. A lecture I watched on late-night TV recently coined the term 'democratic excess' for me. A professor of political science in Toronto said this refers to perfectly legal acts passed by a legislature, or government regulations, that in fact are not in the general public interest but mainly serve narrow political, sectarian or the legislators' own ends.

The fragmentation of our polity yields such fragile majorities on the floor of any House that democratic excess is rampant and no difficult decisions get taken. Yet all the decisions needed to address our problems are difficult ones. Impasse. This is true and the current fate of today's Mumbai.

A very large proportion of public life has been made to serve sectarian ends, to the point where a world city is today a provincial backwater, rapidly dwindling in any stature at all, except possibly in cricket. Even there, the Ranji Trophy, which had taken up more or less permanent residence in the showcases of the Cricket Club of India, travels to other states with worrisome frequency.

The other difference from the past is Mumbai's lawlessness. This does mean the cops and robbers aspect, guns and gangs. But perhaps more importantly, we speak of a privileged political class whom nothing can touch, flouting of municipal and police regulations with impunity, disregard even of High Court orders when it affects political lobbies, arbitrary transfers of officers and officials. We have laws whose only articles are defined by corruption. There is a breakdown of governance. The city could not fail to pay the price.

Tragically, Mumbai's politics and its economics are on a collision course. In the last four years, the growth rate of Mumbai's GDP has fallen well below India's and even Maharashtra's. Meanwhile, political leaders talk merely of slum 'regularization', and 'Mee Mumbaikar'! That's their response to the troubles of India's 'Locomotive City', its 'Money Metropolis'.

Per capita income in the city has dropped dramatically. Population has ballooned but jobs have simply not kept pace. Against a national average of 40% employment in the informal sector, something like 70% of the employed in the city are hawkers, casual labourers or workers in anything but regulated employment. Socioeconomic experts note the obvious: the city's social fabric is under increasing tension with so many on the fringe of joblessness.

At the same time, businesses and head offices are leaving Mumbai for Dubai and Singapore, now even Hyderabad and Bangalore. Already, of Rs 40,000 crore that Mumbai contributes to state and central revenues, only some 16% comes back.

A city is the sum of its economic opportunities and quality of life. Mumbai finds less and less favour internationally. In a quality of life rating by *Forbes*, we are ranked as low as 163 out of 218 cities worldwide. In another survey, on what is called the Hardship Index, we were near the bottom, 124th out of 130 cities.

And why indeed not? The city's infrastructure is strained. Water supply and sanitation are in bad shape. Where this was once the country's best served city for transport, jammed suburban trains and overcrowded buses deliver exhausted people to their jobs in the morning. Yet the increase in cars far outstrips any increase in road kilometres. Traffic congests, there are problems of mobility and some of the lowest average speeds of vehicles on the street in Asian and world class cities. The impact on the air that the city breathes can be imagined.

Housing? Mumbai is one of the most expensive cities in the world for business and residential space, but you get a poor deal in quality of housing. Nearly three-quarters of our households live in a single room. Over half the population lives in slums, more than in any Asian or world class city.

We have destroyed India's cutting-edge city of the fifties. We have slowly got used to a city that works less and less well. But today's national economies depend on how well their cities work. If Mumbai and India are to get anywhere, Mumbai must get globally competitive, and we are nowhere there.

The situation is of course by no means hopeless. Hope lies in the city's financial and commercial importance. The Reserve Bank and State Bank headquarters are here, as are those of virtually every major commercial bank. The main stock and commodity exchanges are here. There are more head offices of the country's top 100 corporations located here than in any other city. All of this is beginning to generate the jobs that the city's people need so desperately. The pace must double. The entertainment industries including cinema (Bollywood!), of which Mumbai is the informal capital, show no signs of decelerating growth, despite piracy and short-sighted tax policies. The information and software industries are as full of promise and challenge as ever they were, needing perhaps midcourse corrections in some sectors which they are well able to handle.

It is these 'new' industries that turn the spotlight on to the city's most precious and promising resource, its young people. Their energy and talent are if anything more surprising than ever before. The competition is greater. You've simply got to be better. But all of this demands discussion at another time and place. I could not bring the present piece to a better pause than with words from that quintessentially Bombay voice, Behram Contractor, the unforgettable 'Busy Bee', first of *The Evening News of India*, then *Mid-day* and finally of *Afternoon Courier and Despatch*, all city eveningers.

'I have lived in Mumbai all my life, and in Bombay before that. I have made many permanent friends. Most of the time I am not aware of their communal identities, as most of the time I am not aware whether I am eating a vegetarian or a non-vegetarian meal. It is like travelling in a crowded railway compartment in the morning, we are all passengers, and we are all going to Churchgate.'

A private view

VINOD MEHTA

FOR me it is virtually impossible to write about Bombay with objectivity or that much vaunted journalistic virtue, balance. Therefore, for those reading this paean, a declaration of interest on my part must be taken as given. I am no historian or biographer of great cities like Geoffrey Moorhouse or Gillian Tindall, whose *City of Gold* is a worthy classic. Neither does the architectural magnificence or melting pot character of the city seduce me. (Melting pots are generally unpleasant.) Bollywood hardly existed in my consciousness – despite one disastrous foray in attempting to put together a biography of Meena Kumari – and in a sojourn of nearly 25 years, I perhaps went to three film parties and hardly knew any film folk.

Nor am I unmindful of the intellectual, social and civic decline of Bombay. Some weeks ago, an issue of *The Economic Times* copiously charted what a sorry mess Bombay had become and why it was no longer the first, or second, or even the third choice of foreign capital wishing to park itself in India. Industrialists with a vested interest in the city noted with shock and disgust how 'Product' Bombay had deteriorated. The remedies they offered were useful from their limited perspective.

I dispute none of the above. In fact, when I visit friends (alas, they are meeting their Maker at an alarming rate!) in Bombay, at some point of time the conversation inevitably turns to the physical and existential decay of their metropolis. The quiet, wise and serene Frank Simoes, who sadly is no longer with us, maintained mischievously that all of us '60s and '70s Bombaywallahs created a phantom city in our mind. It never existed. Whereupon Frank was instantly pounced upon, making him spend the rest of the afternoon/night drinking even more large vodkas.

For myself, an arriviste of the '70s, phantom Bombay did exist. I lived in the 'phantom' and profited from it hugely. Three cities, Lucknow, London and Bombay, have helped shape my character and personality. Of the three, I owe Bombay the most..

A hack like me faces enormous difficulty capturing the essence or mood of a mammoth, sprawling city which possesses at once money, culture and history. (I am more accustomed to dissecting the boring, internecine struggles in the BJP.) At the best of times these things are ineffable, undefinable. Ernest Hemingway's *Moveable Feast*, i.e., Paris, is now seen as Second World War nostalgia. Those who eulogise London should read George Orwell's *Down and Out*. Cities, like people, are rooted in time and place and context. Nothing is permanent. Everything lies in the eye of the beholder.

My story is simply told. Indeed, it is (and certainly in the '60s and '70s it was) a commonplace. I arrived with not many rupees, with no qualifications, with no letter of recommendation, with no friends, with no place to live. All I had was an exaggerated notion of my own worth and an ambition the size of Boribunder. Sounds familiar?

I lived close to a quarter-of-a-century in Bombay and made something of a name as a journalist. I am convinced, totally and utterly convinced, that in any other city of our inestimable country, the opportunity to progress from novice to professional to mini-success would have been infinitely harder to obtain, if not impossible.

When I fled in late 1989, chased by menacing crowds, I had every reason to feel bitter, humiliated and angry. Happily, the anger and bitterness soon passed. Only the pleasure and an overwhelming sense of gratitude remain.

Graham Greene once observed that a person should be judged by his enmities as well as his friendships. Two enemies in nearly 25 years is not a bad record! I refer in my case to Bal Thackeray and Sharad Pawar. Thackeray is practically a universal enemy, so his hostility one wears like a badge of honour, but Pawar still has a few friends left. Fortunately, I am not one of them. These two gentlemen worked hard to run me out of Mumbai. They succeeded. (In another number of *Seminar*, if there is any interest, I could recount the details of my forced exile.)

Other matters aside, one's love or loathing for a city depends largely on the quality of time spent in it. Except for the aforementioned 30-odd days in 1989, I cannot think of a period when I was (seriously) unhappy or depressed or bitter in Bombay. There were times I had no job, there were times I had virtually no money, there were times when my prospects appeared bleaker than those of the current BJP government. Happily, I had so much to be thankful for, so many pleasant memories both at work and play, so much generosity showered on me by anonymous folks, that the bad times hardly registered. The kindness of strangers through which Tennessee Williams survived, I experienced almost on a daily basis.

In Delhi, where I presently reside, failure dogs you; people known and unknown constantly wait for it to strike you. In Bombay, failure is considered the path to eventual success; in Delhi failure is considered the path to (hopefully) more failure. It is worshipped for its own sake.

When I read about so-and-so film star in the dumps in Bombay with five flops in a row, instinct and experience tell me that if he or she has a gram of talent their sixth film will be a hit and the wonderful people of Bombay (trade and public alike) will immediately forgive his/her string of disasters and pronounce the individual a 'star' again. The crucial and perhaps most significant difference between Delhi and Bombay is that Delhi celebrates failure while Bombay celebrates success.

India's capital is not a warm or large-hearted metropolis. It is mean-spirited. In my own profession, which is journalism, the degree of back biting, malice, carefully choreographed disinformation and plain envy has to be experienced to be believed. Naturally, upwardly mobile scribes are, as everywhere, aggressively competitive, determined to reach the No.1 position. In this town, however, there is a special and nasty edge to the race for the top, which is manifested in the belittling and running-down of accomplishment. Running down people, in fact, is an industry here.

Since I am still a bit of an outsider in Delhi, I am unfamiliar with how precisely the game is played, but I can assure you, kind words and fond thoughts and graceful acceptance of achievement are more or less invisible. Whenever four or five people are gathered together beneath Lutyens' stylish landscape, dollops of malice, you can be pretty certain, is being freely dispensed. And relished.

When I was destitute and desolate in Mumbai, which was quite often, I would come across complete strangers on the street or at parties. They would say something like: 'I heard about your sacking, but don't worry you will get another paper to edit soon.' After quitting *The Indian Post* in 1988, I received huge amounts of mail from fellow journalists expressing sympathy and regret. When I resigned from *The Pioneer* in Delhi in 1994 there was thundering silence mixed with quiet rejoicing.

I left Mumbai in late 1989 and till last year at least each time I returned, many friends informed me that the Bombay I lived in is dead. The spirit of tolerance is dead and has been replaced by a spirit of hatred. Now people, literally and metaphorically, prefer to live exclusively in their small or big patch. Culture is ugly, politics is ugly, the city is being made ugly, people-to-people relationships are ugly. And ugliest of all: no one is fighting back. I cannot really comment on the accuracy of the diagnosis. I hope, and I suspect, it is slightly exaggerated. We live in ugly times, therefore Bombay cannot expect to remain uncontaminated.

All Mumbaikars, and I count myself as one of them, have a responsibility to preserve and nourish Bombay's big heart, its unrivalled generosity, its welcome to those ready to chance their ambition. The Shiv Sena, of course, is the principal adversary of such an enterprise. The SS, alas, is not the city's only foe. There is, unfortunately, a creeping complacency in the citizenry, a resignation, a feeling that nothing can be done.

Bombay was once the abode of alert and vigilant civic citizens. Where are the elegant Parsi ladies rescuing sick pigeons? Where are the Friends of the Trees?

Why don't we see more initiatives like Save the Oval campaign? Not so long ago, Bombay was packed with talented, enterprising, dedicated and useful eccentrics – why have they gone underground? When the aristocracy, in terms of city pride, in any city retreats, the merchants of vulgarity take over.

Before Bombay became Mumbai, the city belonged to nobody and everybody. Like millions, when I arrived with a single hundred rupee note in my pocket and many crazy ideas in my head, I stayed in a seedy hotel on Wodehouse Road called Buckley Court. Each character who lived there was worthy of a Conrad short story, if not a full novel. At the breakfast table and at the famous 'Olympia' restaurant in Colaba late at night, mind boggling plans and strategies used to be thrown up and discussed furiously. (An exiled Armenian lady and her son were plotting an armed rebellion from the hotel.) Yet, frivolity or diversion was not our purpose. The city gave space for wild imagination and, most crucially, provided numerous instances of people who from hotels like Buckley Court had 'made it big'. Cranks and eccentrics were welcome; they too could try and court the bitch goddess.

Anyone who has lived and mingled in Bombay must record how his precious time spent there was made immeasurably richer by interaction and discourse with the rank and file of two communities – the Parsis and the Goans. These extraordinary, carefree, gifted, generous, zany residents' contribution, not just to commerce, but to the gaiety of life in the city cannot be over-emphasised.

Delhi dreams too – I know lots of individuals dreaming of becoming cabinet ministers – but the schemes here are shady and the strategies invariably involve double-crossing and blackmail. In Bombay, miraculously, dreaming was open, legitimate, indeed frequently mandatory. Your friends and relatives encouraged you to dream – and dream on a mega scale. That glorious mix of fantasy and fact cannot be allowed to die.

I interrupt here for some breaking news. At the end of May this year on a brief visit to Bombay, I found the citizens more or less at peace. The city has come to terms with its No. 2 status as far as wealth, power and influence are concerned. That there is more disposable income in Delhi – 'it is a trader's city' is mentioned without disrespect – is freely conceded, while the itinerant visitor from India's capital is treated with a mixture of admiration and awe. Ten years ago it was pure contempt.

But there is a more profound change. The population of Bombay seems less neurotic, less paranoid. It does not constantly look over its shoulder. And for this happy state of affairs, one must be grateful to the steady decline and influence of the single most corrosive, corrupting and regressive force in Bombay, i.e., the Shiv Sena. When the history of the great metropolis is rewritten, the Shiv Sena will get more than a passing mention.

More than the crude and frequently comical spectacles of fascism and totalitarianism, Shri Bal Thackeray sought to destroy the indomitable spirit and cosmopolitan culture of Bombay – and he nearly succeeded. He was stopped in his tracks by his strong tendency to self-destruct and, more crucially, by the common sense of middle-class Maharashtrians who Thackeray had briefly won over. When Balasaheb meets the 'Grim Reaper', he will leave behind a party in shambles. Its disintegration is imminent. A fact for which we must all rejoice.

Bombay may never fully regain its '60s glory, but for me and for millions, it will remain the city which taught us everything we know.

Blitz's Bombay

GYAN PRAKASH

GROWING up in Patna during the 1960s, I remember the weekly arrival of the *Blitz*. When my father returned after a full day at the High Court, he would leaf through the day's mail, pluck the weekly tabloid from Bombay wrapped in its sleeve of recycled brown paper, and retreat with it to his bedroom. After changing out of his court attire, he relaxed on the bed and waited for the servant to bring his tea. As my mother poured him tea, he began devouring the sensational accounts of national and international skullduggery. His face, hidden behind the tabloid held high in his hands, only appeared from time to time to sip his tea.

Nothing interrupted his attention, not even my mother's ritual commentary on the day's routine events and family gossip. Aside from the occasional polite 'hmms' directed at my mother, my father broke his silent attention only when he read aloud in shock the sensational headlines – 'CIA Jamboree in New Delhi.' I sat opposite, drinking my milk while I stole a glance at the last page where, beside the K.A. Abbas column, a pinup greeted the reader with a witty caption – 'Nalini makes a winsome bather, But will someone blow off the lather!'

As soon as my father was done reading, I would grab it and withdraw to some place quiet to mostly look at – not read – the spunky tabloid's loud and screaming captions and telling photographs. The paper's quality was coarse and the pictures grainy, but there was visual drama on Blitz's pages. Together, the text and graphics evoked an image of an expansive and exciting life and that my adolescent mind associated with the exciting city of its publication – Bombay.

Blitz first appeared on 1st February 1941. It was founded by R.K. Karanjia, who had earlier worked at *The Times of India*, and had briefly edited the *Sunday Standard* and the short-lived *Morning Standard*. He assembled a group that comprised three others: Dinkar V. Nadkarni, who had earned a reputation in journalism by penning sensational crime stories in the *Bombay Sentinel*, edited by the veteran B.G. Horniman; Zahir Babar Kureishi, who wrote a popular column under the pen-name of ZABAK; and Nadir Boman-Behram, who was to look after the advertizing and business side of things.

All four resigned from the Standard and launched the new tabloid from an old Apollo Street building in the Fort. The inaugural issue introduced the tabloid as 'Our BLITZ, India's BLITZ against Hitler.'[1] Within four months of the inaugural issue, the circulation had reached 20,000; twenty-five years later, the 'people's paper' claimed a readership of one million.[2]

It was not entirely fortuitous that Bombay was the successful launching pad for Blitz. Well before India's independence, Bombay was the most dynamic and modern Indian city. Calcutta and Madras were also important cities, but Bombay was unique. Among urban centres that had grown up under the *raj*, it was the only one where Indians – most notably the Parsis and Gujarati Hindus and Jains – had significant stakes in its industry, finance and banking. Also, unlike other cities, its thriving capitalist industry and finance outweighed the importance of the government bureaucracy.

1. 'To Our Readers', 1 February 1941,' cited in *Blitz*, 25 February 1961, p. 7.
2. 'Mighty All-party Rally Felicitates Editor Karanjia', *Blitz*, 27 February 1965, p. 3.

This did not change after independence; while New Delhi attracted politicians and political fixers, people from all over India washed up on the island city looking for jobs and opportunities. Bombay became known for its vitality and diversity during the fifties and the sixties. Although Marathi-speakers formed the single-largest group, no regional culture dominated the city's cultural and social life. A range of religious communities – Hindus, Muslims, Christians, Jains, Zoroastrians, and Jews – and linguistic groups – Marathi, Konkani, Hindi, Urdu, and Telugu speakers, and many others made up the urban mix.

Writers and intellectuals from North India flocked to the city to work in journalism and in the film industry; and educated men journeyed from South India to find work in shipping, banking, and commercial establishments. The partition of British India was a blow to the city's Muslim community and its cosmopolitan air, but the tumult also brought a huge influx of refugees, raising Bombay's population from 1.4 million in 1941 to 2.3 million in 1951.[3]

This bustling, island city was a modern city with all its contradictions. A place of commerce and free enterprise, bourgeois prosperity and brutal exploitation lived cheek by jowl in the city. If Bombay boasted of the posh Malabar Hill, Cuffe Parade, and the panorama of Marine Drive where the legendary merchant princes and textile magnates lived, it was also known for its tightly-packed *chawls* and pavements that the poor called home.

A culture of money, for which Bombay was legendary, held together these glaring disparities and contradictions. Its capitalist economy shaped Bombay's complex social architecture that housed industrialists, bankers, investors, wage workers, the salaried masses, casual labourers, owners and employees in retail businesses, journalists, teachers, artists, writers, architects, engineers, doctors, administrators, politicians, and criminals. The city was society, and

3. Meera Kosambi, *Bombay in Transition: The Growth and Social Ecology of a Colonial City, 1880-1980*. Almqvist and Wiksell International, Stockholm, 1986, p. 165.

Bombay's social life was lived in spaces and in rhythms of work and leisure that signified modernity.

Not the least important of these spaces was an active public sphere serviced by newspapers, civic leaders, and trade unions and political parties of different ideological stripes. This was the modern city of the late colonial and early post-independence era that acquired a classic image in the representations of Hindi cinema of the period.

Blitz both inhabited this milieu and gave it a characteristic definition. As a newsweekly, it drew on Bombay's highly developed bourgeois public sphere. A key element of this sphere was the city's newspapers in which Bombay's public life appeared as news and photographs. As is the case with all newspapers, Bombay's press also served a crucial function in making the city legible.

Typically, newspaper readers confront their public world in reports on politics and economics, descriptions of social engagements, crime stories, announcements of job vacancies and tender notices, advertizements of products and entertainment, film and theatre reviews, and accounts of sporting events. In an important sense, newspapers actually bring the public sphere to life for their readers, and function as agents of acting upon it. In modern city life, it has been said that the secular ritual of reading newspaper replaces the morning prayer.

Of course, it is safe to say that Bombay's illiterate and poor citizens were free of this secular ritual. For this reason, the public life rendered real by the newspapers was also beyond them. What is more, English dominated the lettered world brought into view by newspapers. In this elitist English-scripted public world, *The Times of India* was pre-eminent. But a colonial genealogy burdened *The Times*. The *Bombay Chronicle* was nationalist, but sober. It was in this context that Blitz appeared in an effort to break open the elite public life with a radical ideology and spunky writing. Accepting the notion of public life as the key arena of politics, the tabloid mined it for its radical potential, believing that hard-hitting, two-fisted reports could make a political difference.

Central to Blitz's self-representation as a radical, people's paper was its tabloid form. The tabloid is a classic urban form that seeks to render legible the anonymous reality of everyday life in the modern metropolis in its bold and sensational headlines. As a tabloid, then, Blitz dispensed with the convention of dispassionate observation and balanced opinion, and adopted a charged tone from the very beginning. It took on the role of a social investigator that dug beneath the surface of everyday life to ferret out the hidden truth that it announced loudly on its pages. The weekly revelled in its self-proclaimed role as a racket-buster, exposing truths concealed by the powerful.

In 1945, for example, D.V. Nadkarni, Blitz's chief 'racket buster', wrote a series of sensational stories on the textile shortage. These accounts claimed to uncover the hidden hand of the big wholesale dealers who, with the alleged help of government officials, were hoarding the stocks to drive up the price while representing it as the product of a natural scarcity.[4]

This was not unusual. Week after week, Blitz exposed truths allegedly buried beneath the surface of random and fragmentary events. The embezzlement of public funds, prostitution rackets, sordid stories of seduction and sex in the name of spiritualism, dark political designs behind high-sounding rhetoric, and the fleecing of the poor by rich industrialists and property developers were staples in the weekly. Even the sports column, called 'Knock Out', took on the racket-busting posture. It was written by A.F.S. Talyarkhan, whose bearded, pipe-in-mouth, face on the page appeared to lend gravity to the charges of malfeasance he made against sports authorities. The poor performance of Indian athletes in international competitions, it turned out, could be explained by petty squabbles and power-grabbing by officials behind the scenes.

In Blitz's world, there was nothing mysterious about reality. Once it had cleared the mist of the surface-level mystery and decoded the outward face of events, the exposed reality always appeared rational –

4. Cited in 'The Racket-Buster', *Blitz*, 25 February 1961, p. 13.

a product of relentlessly instrumental and banal pursuits of money and power. The scandal lay in the fact that people wrapped their ruthlessly rational motivations and actions in tissues of lies and deceptions. This required a careful scrutiny of the misleading exteriority of events. The journalist had to act as a detective and plunge into the rough and tumble of life. He examined seemingly disconnected fragments to decipher hidden connections and detect clues to the underlying reality. In this process, the journalist-as-detective functioned as an author who produced written and illustrative political and social texts that claimed to depict modernity's imperceptible reality.

Bombay acquired a textual and photographic face in the news accounts and images that sought to represent the reality in its surface-level expressions. No grand philosophy or concept defined this depiction of reality. Rather, the tabloid identified the phenomena in the empirical material itself, in the exemplary spaces and activities of modern life. It traced the contours of Bombay's daily life on its streets and neighbourhoods, restaurants and cinema theatres, textile factories and neighbourhoods, docks and shipping offices, and municipal institutions and public parks. Warnings of 'Death-Trap for Promenaders at Marine Drive Seafront,'[5] exposures of 'Super-Market in Sex: Where Vice is sold on Department-Store Basis!'[6] or 'Bombay Municipality Creates Slums'[7] formed the stuff of Blitz's Bombay.

These stories of the city's dark side did not signify cultural pessimism or despair. If anything, Blitz always expressed supreme confidence in modern life. Showing no nostalgia for the imagined harmony of the countryside, it openly embraced the gritty, conflict-ridden, urban milieu of Bombay. While it uncovered tales of greed for money and power, it also provided glamorous accounts of film personalities, and celebrated popular struggles for justice.

On its pages, the city appeared as an immense and exciting mix of multi-layered, contradictory, and restless lives. Everything seemed

5. *Blitz*, 2 December 1961, p. 3.

6. Ibid., p. 17.

7. Ibid., 13 March 1965, p. 8.

to be in motion. Fortunes were being made and lost, swindles were being plotted and exposed, and big dreams were being dreamt and shattered. People jostled for space, and they heroically struggled for survival and justice. Against the shadow of its dark side, Bombay's metropolitan life glittered on the Blitz pages.

Among its many stories on the city, there was one that came to define Blitz and encapsulated its titillating representation of Bombay's metropolitan life. This story related to the Nanavati case, and its central actors were Commander Kawas Manekshaw Nanavati, a Parsi naval officer; his English wife Sylvia; and a rich Sindhi playboy, Prem Ahuja. On 27th April 1959, Sylvia confessed to her 37 year old husband that she had been having an affair with Ahuja.

After lunch in his Cuffe Parade home, Nanavati dropped off his wife, his two children, and a neighbour's child at the Metro Cinema for the afternoon show of *Tom Thumb*. From there, he proceeded to his ship 'Mysore' where he obtained a revolver and six rounds of ammunition, and then drove to the Universal Motors office on Pedder Road. Upon learning that Ahuja, the car dealership's manager, had not returned from lunch, Nanavati drove to his wife's lover's flat in 'Jeevan Jyoti' (The Flame of Life) on Malabar Hill. The naval officer entered the flat, an argument followed, three shots rang out, and Ahuja lay dead.

Soon afterwards, Nanavati drove to the naval authorities, and surrendered. In the trial, Nanavati claimed that Ahuja was killed unintentionally when the two men struggled for the gun. The jury acquitted him, but the Sessions Court judge, dissatisfied with the verdict, referred the case to the High Court. The High Court convicted him of murder and sentenced him to life imprisonment, a decision that the Supreme Court confirmed. Eventually, he was pardoned by the President, and the Nanavati family migrated to Canada.

This, in a nutshell, was the Nanavati case. In fact, it became much more as soon as the trial opened in the Sessions Court on 13 October 1959. None did more to make a routine murder trial into a classic story of Bombay's bourgeois life than the Blitz. As soon as the trial began, Blitz published nine pages of what it called a pictorial record of the case with a bold, front-page headline 'Three Shots That Shook the Nation.'[8] With detailed text accompanying the photographs of the main *dramatis personae*, the homicide scene, the witnesses, and attorneys, it made the Nanavati case its top story.

For the next two years that the Nanavati case moved up the ladder of courts, its spotlight remained intensely focused on the case. It offered full-throated support to Nanavati, unfailingly portraying him as a handsome, upright, and patriotic officer. Almost always publishing his photograph in his smart naval uniform, Nanavati was depicted as a wronged husband. Sylvia, who had become a guilt-ridden, remorseful wife during the trial, was portrayed as a beautiful, blue-eyed, and guileless 28 year old cynically seduced by an unscrupulous playboy. Blitz ran a tireless campaign for Nanavati's acquittal. After his conviction, it held public meetings, and conducted signature campaigns to secure a pardon. Karanjia often wrote, defending Nanavati by suggesting that while the naval officer represented middle-class, family values, Ahuja symbolized the corrupt, amorality of the upper-class minority.[9]

As Blitz emblazoned its pages with Nanavati's defense, it also turned the case into a compelling story of love, betrayal and homicide. The tabloid told its readers about the romance and marriage of the dashing Bombay-born naval officer and the pretty Sylvia in England. It affixed on their minds Bombay's social geography by mentioning the posh Cuffe Parade and Malabar Hill as the locus for the drama of adultery and murder. These, in addition to accounts of how and where Ahuja and Sylvia met and carried on their affair, the publication of their love letters, and details about the Nanavatis' and Ahuja's daily lives, succeeded in portraying the Nanavati case as an exotic story set in Bombay.

In broadcasting a Bombay story nationally, Blitz disseminated an image of the city nationwide. A few years later, a Hindi film very

8. Ibid., 24 October 1959.

9. 'Defence of Nanavati!', ibid., 19 March 1960, p. 1.

loosely based on the Nanavati case, *Yeh Raaste Hain Pyaar Ke*, starring Sunil Dutt, Leela Naidu and Rehman, was released. An echo of Blitz's portrayal of the case is identifiable in the film, but it was faint and entirely forgettable. Blitz, on the other hand, had carried out its campaign with great panache. It had taken a quotidian city episode and transformed it into a story for consumption in the bourgeois mass culture throughout India. Implicit in its energetic coverage of the Nanavati case was the confidence both in the wider significance of a Bombay story and in the importance of the bourgeois public sphere. A city paper, Blitz called itself Asia's foremost news magazine. It originated in Bombay, but it reached into the city's rich tradition of public life, gave it a radical content, and then confidently proclaimed its concerns as national.

There was something of Bombay's self-assurance about its modernity in Blitz's attempt to become a medium of mass culture. This was visible from very early on as the tabloid's brash tone was set to orchestrate a relentlessly nationalist line strongly inflected by leftist themes. An unapologetic supporter of Nehru, it vigorously championed secularism, supported socialism and planning, denounced capitalism, and poured scorn on right wing and communal politicians. It coupled this ideology with a leftist internationalism. It lauded Afro-Asian solidarity against the capitalist West – the Egyptian President Nasser was its hero – and it loudly and regularly unveiled dark, CIA plots against India and Third World leaders.

The presence of several columnists with communist sympathy on its ranks – Ramesh Sanghvi, A. Raghavan, and K.A. Abbas – contributed to the leftist flavour. Bombay was the headquarters of the Communist Party until the end of the forties. The city's film industry also attracted several communist writers, journalists, artists, and intellectuals. The communist Girni Kamgar Union, which was the most important trade union of the city's textile workers, also added to the leftist presence in Bombay.

While these were undoubtedly important factors, it is also clear that Karanjia revelled in playing the advocate for socialism and the champion of the Third World cause against American interests. A characteristic example of his posture was the front page story in the early sixties headlined 'Editor Karanjia Crashed U.S. Curtain into Cuba.'[10] The report, datelined from Havana, triumphantly noted Karanjia's arrival in Cuba at Fidel Castro's invitation in spite of the obstruction placed by the denial of a transit visa by the US to permit him to fly via New York. When Nasser visited the city in 1960, Blitz declared: 'President Nasser Captivates the Heart of Bombay!'[11] Five years later, Nasser bestowed Karanjia with the highest award given to a foreigner. Exultantly, Blitz reported that despite torrential rain thousands of Bombay's citizens turned out to felicitate Karanjia.[12]

The editor's ideology and personality defined the tabloid. Belonging to the minority Parsi community, Karanjia's commitment to secular politics was understandable. But he combined secular, modern values with a full-blooded anti-imperialism that was not common among the Parsis. In this respect, Karanjia's political views closely echoed those of his idol, Nehru, who also saw a robust national identity and anti-imperialist cosmopolitanism as complementary. Indeed, the endorsement of Afro-Asian solidarity, the admiration for the Soviet Union and the distrust of the United States, and the support for socialism and planning formed parts of an ideology that was widely shared in the decolonized world during the fifties and sixties. So, Karanjia was not alone in espousing these ideas; like the intelligentsia in many other newly independent Third World nations, he too envisioned the fulfillment of modern nationhood in anti-imperialist internationalism and socialism.

But Karanjia's journalistic creation was no ordinary left-nationalist fare. Throughout its existence under its flamboyant editor, Blitz's signature was its muckraking, over-the top stories calculated to provoke and enrage. It thrived on controversy, and Karanjia was frequently embroiled in defamation suits, which the tabloid wore

10. *Blitz*, 25 June 1960, p. 1. Below the main story was another headline, 'Did US Spy Chief Dulles Meet [the Naga leader] Phizo?'

11. Ibid., 16 April 1960, p. 15.

12. Festival of Indo-Arab Amity', *Blitz*, 3 July 1965.

as a badge of honour and showcased on its pages even when it lost. Its opinions were full-throated, and its likes and dislikes of political personalities and parties were unconcealed.

Thus, Blitz screamed 'Lies, Mr. Patil – black, bald lies!' denouncing the right-wing Congress leader, S.K. Patil.[13] The occasion was the parliamentary election campaign of 1967 in Bombay. Krishna Menon, denied nomination by the Congress at the behest of leaders including S.K. Patil, had joined the electoral fray as an independent candidate supported by the Left. Blitz hailed Menon as a socialist, and offered enthusiastic support to his candidacy from North Bombay. Its front page even proclaimed 'Menon Has Won' in bold headlines even before the election had occurred, explaining it as a rising crescendo of public opinion.[14]

When he lost the election, Blitz thundered 'Rape of the Ballot Box', followed by the subtitle, 'Patil, Barve and SS Out-Hitlered Hitler.'[15] 'SS' referred to Bal Thackeray's Shiv Sena, which, according to Blitz, had terrorized voters, particularly South Indians whom the new nativist party had already made targets of its violent campaign. The tabloid was unrelenting in exposing the Shiv Sena's violent tactics. Issue after issue, it spotlighted the Sena's terror politics.

Blitz's opposition to the Shiv Sena was not just due to electoral reasons; the Sena fundamentally negated Blitz's cosmopolitanism. Referring to the hoodlum tactics of the Sena, Karanjia wrote: 'Never before was this proud city, with its splendid cosmopolitan traditions and secular culture, so brutally soiled, shamed, violated and dishonoured as today.'[16] Significantly, Blitz had hailed the creation of Maharashtra, and had lauded Shivaji as a Maharashtrian symbol,[17] and

13. Ibid., 21 January 1967, p. 1.
14. Ibid., 18 February 1967, p. 1.
15. Ibid., 25 February 1967, p. 1.
16. Ibid., 'Citizens' Ultimatum to Patil, Barve, Shah and Co: Disown Shiv Sena – or Quit Bombay!' 4 February 1967, p. 1.
17. See, for example, the 23 April 1960 issue that welcomed the creation of the new state, and paid rich tributes to Shivaji's legacy.

the Left had played a leading role in the struggle for the new linguistic state.

But once the Shiv Sena twisted the desire for linguistic identity into a violent drive for nativist supremacy, Blitz's Bombay became endangered. As the Sena pummeled the communist trade unions, the Congress colluded with Bal Thackeray, and the politician-builder-underworld nexus increasingly invaded Bombay politics during the seventies, the ground beneath the tabloid shifted. It continued publication through the seventies and eighties, and even after being bought by Vijay Mallya in 1996, but the tabloid's modernist vision had lost its confident, radical tone at the end of the sixties.

The waning of Blitz's self-assured modernism signalled the diminishing appeal of the Nehruvian vision, and formed part of a larger historical transformation. When I visited Patna on holidays from college in Delhi during the early seventies, I noticed that our household in Patna had remained a loyal subscriber. My father continued his weekly routine of unwinding from work with Blitz, but it seemed more habit than interest. I too found the tabloid less alluring. Perhaps my father's concerns were focused elsewhere, and I had also grown up and moved on. But the tabloid had also changed. The coverage was more obsessively political, and the anti-establishment tone rang hollow in view of its full-throated support for Indira Gandhi's cynical rhetoric of socialism.

Most of all, Blitz's Bombay had lost its shine. The city appeared as a place of shrill political rhetoric and deep social divisions. Corruption, and violence had become endemic, and the air was pessimistic. This presented a striking contrast to the optimistic image of Bombay as the promised city of modernity that Blitz had so effectively disseminated across India during the fifties and sixties. It is tempting to view this change nostalgically, and represent it as the death of the cosmopolitan Bombay.

In fact, what died was Blitz's idea of Bombay. It was an elitist ideal, one that rested on a deep belief in the authority and centrality of the bourgeois public sphere, law, and the modern nation-state.

This elitist imagination may have lost its compelling appeal with the demise of the Nehruvian vision, but underlying Blitz's representation of Bombay was the projection of the city as modern society – the city was made to stand for the promise of modern conditions of freedom and democracy in post-colonial India. In an important sense, this remains an urgent issue today.

The free for all city

CYRUS GUZDER

'Commoners here by thousands float
And jostle one another down
Each paddling in his leaky boat
And here they fish for gold; or drown.'

Jonathan Swift

'Bombay is a great city – but a terrible place!' Charles Correa's famous remark encapsulates the difficulty of defining the essential spirit of Bombay. No simple description of the city is adequate – the place is just too complex, too diverse. For the last 50 years, this island city has suffered an explosion of growth and change, spurred on not by the singular vision or actions of a great leader but by a messy organic expansion, where every assumption of the city's planners is overtaken by events, and most reserved spaces for public amenities are giving way to encroachments, squatter-colonies for the poor or illegal buildings for the better off.

Writers, filmmakers and poets have all struggled to describe this phenomenon. Pico Iyer, in his evocative account of Bombay (called

'Hobson-Jobson on the Streets') saw the city as 'some mythical monster on the move, at dawn and dusk at the same time.' It is impossible not to feel the sizzle of our Wall Street, the stench of urine and garbage, the glitter of Bollywood whose beautiful faces oversee the city from cinema hoardings everywhere, the new Shanghai rising in the Bandra-Kurla Banking District, the 13 feet by 13 feet regulation *kholis* in the textile mill *chawls*, even smaller living spaces in the innumerable slums, hawkers on every busy street, having displaced customers from shops on the very same pavement now displacing each other in raucous defiance of every authority.

But, everywhere, you see in this city that 'as with its horrors, so are its wonders beyond reason.' That, everywhere, in all but the most wretched situations, 'good cheer is in constant collision with enterprise.'

A city that is so noisy day and night, whose new buildings are so drab, which looks so dreary during the rains, which inflicts so much hardship on its people – has still captured their souls in some inexplicable way. This adversity seems to have fuelled extraordinary energy among the people. To an outsider, the city often seems a 'kaleidoscope of colours, sounds and images' – a constant carnival parade – a chaotic 'jostling of clangorous, technicolour profusion.'

But Bombay is truly a city of paradoxes, where every description, and its opposite, find a place. In *Midnight's Children*, Rushdie's Salmaan, returned from Rawalpindi to Bombay, is excited by 'the rainbow riot of the city.' Yet Rohinton Mistry's anti-hero finds the same Bombay 'brown and weary and unhappy.' Even Satyajit Ray could not help himself from comparing Bombay to a highly painted courtesan '...at once seductive and revolting.'

Languages, too, reflect the bitter-sweet hybrids of their speakers (Cross *Maidan*, Apollo *Bunder*, *Mahalaxmi* Race Course, *Mahatma Gandhi* Road, meeting *Wellington* Circle on the way to *Chhatrapati Shivaji* Terminus). The cohabitation of so many communities (in which city in the world can you go to the theatre in four or five languages?) and their festivals, their cuisine (Jain, Chinese or Mexican *bhel puri* at Vithal's; *dosas* with Goa prawn curry filling at Dosa Diner; *kesar pista masala* cassata at Dinshaw's Ice Cream Parlors) – all making it clear that we should now avoid the cliché that Bombay is a 'melting pot' of so many different cultures.

Far from its different communities getting melted down into one brown stew, so many pots can be seen simmering away separately on their respective *choolahs* flavouring our atmosphere with a unique blend of scents and odours. Gieve Patel, a poet from Bombay, described these on a visit to one of our railway stations in his poem 'Bombay Central':

> 'the odour does not offend...
> an amalgam of diesel oil, hot steel, cool rails,
> lights and shadow, human sweat,
> metallic distillations, dung;
> newspaper ink, Parle's gluco biscuits
> all hitting the nostrils as one singular, atmospheric thing
> seeping into your clothing.'

Bombay is not an ancient city. Its frenetic growth has been crammed into just the last three centuries, one influx of persons, one wave of change following swiftly upon the other. The earliest Koli fisher *bastis* and mangrove marshes were first imprinted by armed European traders. Then came waves of immigrants from Gujarat and the Deccan, all the while reclamation filling in the interstices between the many fingers of its low lying islands, so that, in just 200 years (a mere blink of Lord Shiva's eye), that great monster of a land-mass seemed to emerge from the sea like a giant Tyrannosaurus Mumbaikar. On its surface, there was teeming activity, with Imperial governors and Indian civil servants attempting to bring order into this activity; marine, railway and PWD engineers, cotton mill owners, philanthropists, financiers, upcountry politicians and property developers, all appearing and putting down roots.

The city, meanwhile, metamorphoses from south to north. In its mouth, a rough-hewn set of dentures appears in the form of the Marine Drive buildings, later showing the polish and sparkle of the flashy windows of Nariman Point's towers; two deep furrows running northwards across its back – the Central and Western Railway lines – eruptions appear like blisters on its hide in the form of a rash of building construction, some rugged as cement, others flimsy enough to be blown away in a monsoon wind, spreading virulently across the eastern and western suburbs; the only constant feature being the green and furry down covering its broader, upper quarters to the north, crawling with the plant and insect life of the Borivili Park.

Charles Correa laments that the 'great' city Bombay – a world city of three million in the 1950s – has now sunk into a provincial agglomeration of 14 million, where living conditions, despite the glamour of its many tall buildings, have deteriorated steadily for the last 50 years. The most striking aspect of Bombay is that a city that generates more wealth than any other metropolis in India, should have done so little to provide decent housing to more than half its residents. Some seven million people don't have access to a toilet or taps with running water in their 'homes', a cruel euphemism for the 200 square feet space which a family of five or six, on average, occupies.

I therefore held my breath when a wealthy estate-developer friend told me, over dinner last year, that he was going to do something on a grand scale – a big 'gesture' – to make Bombay a better place! His project: to build two 60-storey residential towers as part of a slum clearance scheme in the Tardeo district. This is an old locality where hundreds of three and four storey buildings receive municipal water for just a few hours each day and where, when the rains come, the ancient choked sewers overflow and turn the streets into rivers of floating shit and dead rats. In this area would now rise two of the country's tallest buildings. They would incorporate all the latest features in earthquake proof design, internal fire fighting, eight stories of podium car parking and, of course, high speed lifts, health clubs, a swimming pool, and so on, all now amenities to be taken for granted by the affluent middle class.

I was immediately reminded of how Professor Henri-Claude de Bettignies, an INSEAD professor, begins his annual five-day retreat at Pebble Beach, California, for global CEOs who have come for a 'refresher' on how to cope with the challenges of managing the world's largest corporations. His first slide seems innocuous enough. A couple of glistening skyscrapers, with a helicopter coming in to land atop one of them, finding a place in between the telecom antennae and dishes, beaming no doubt to the far corners of the globe, the instructions of those powerful men, alighting from their large black limousines at the lobby below. A familiar scene to the viewers.

But just below the embankment on which these towering symbols of power stand, are steps that lead down to the edge of an open sewer, where another teeming world resides. A mass of street dwellers' shacks, balanced on the edge of a drain, children squatting in the muck, a bunch of ragpickers sharing a snort of 'coke', all under the watchful eye of a policeman collecting his 'protective' take from the street hawkers. Again, nothing unusual, for his well-travelled audience.

Yet, according to de Bettignies, this is the key issue for global CEOs to ponder. Big corporations need growing markets. What is the future of global business if the steel and glass edifices are being corroded at their foundations by overwhelming numbers of the underprivileged? It's not much different in the countryside, where overwhelming numbers of marginal farmers are dispossessed. Yet these high rise buildings, far from being the solution, seem to increase the gulf between their lofty residents and those condemned to live at ground level.

The 24th anniversary issue of Bombay's *Mid-day* had a touching series on 'How it feels…' (…to have climbed Everest; to have escaped death). The euphoric builder who lives atop his 42-storey creation at Nana Chowk, tells us 'how it feels' to live in Bombay's just built, tallest building: 'The best part is to see the city below, at my feet; even better when it rains and I see the ground through the clouds, as if I am flying.'

But what life do those below enjoy as they contemplate this towering monster whose needs for water will dry up their mains and water hydrants, whose sewage will burst through their manhole covers when it rains heavily, and whose cars keep adding to the gridlock on the roads?

If our estate 'developer' chose to take a morning walk below, perhaps the lines of Nissim Ezekiel might come alive to him:

'Barbaric city, sick with slums,
Deprived of seasons, blessed with rains,
Its hawkers, beggars, iron-lunged,
Processions led by frantic drums'
A million purgatorial lanes,
And child-like masses, many tongued,
Whose wages are in words and crumbs.'[1]

It's sad that a pessimism has now taken deep root in some of Bombay's most creative people. In a February 2002 issue of *Outlook* featuring an article by Darryl D'Monte 'Bye Bye Bombay,' Naushad the Music Director laments; '...the city is in irreversible decline.' 'No hope till we drive out the immigrants,' says Pramod Navalkar. 'City of gold has become city of dross,' says Darryl himself. 'Mumbai is now Slum-bai; it's too late for Mumbai to be saved' complains Vijay Tendulkar. And even Gerson da Cunha, who has launched a courageous public crusade against corrupt candidates in the city's municipal elections, surprises us by his statement: 'Intellectually, the city has blown out its brain!'

For the brightest in Bombay to be so negative is not only a result of the usual dismay with the state of the courts, the police, conservancy and utilities. In Bombay, the deeper concern is that we have lost control of the processes that now drive the city's physical development. For example, the planning regulations have been freed from any ceiling on FSI when re-development of cessed (over 50 years old) buildings is undertaken. That is how just a few old five storey buildings in Nana Chowk, Tardeo, were transmuted into a forty-plus

1. From: 'A Morning Walk', in *Collected Poems 1952-1988* by Nissim Ezekiel. Oxford University Press, 1989.

storey tower. Never mind that it needs considerable sleight of hand to create the paper work to make this possible.

In the case of slum redevelopment, a grossly ill-conceived strategy incentivises builders to rehabilitate slum dwellers free of cost, in return for permission to build and sell (at market prices) real estate, the area of which is related to the slum families re-housed. A Slum Redevelopment Authority was created and given extraordinary powers to give effect to this scheme. No wonder that it has created enormous incentives to inflate the number of slum dwellers so as to increase the amount of free-sale upmarket space; to encourage criminals to substitute genuine slum dwellers by those prepared to pay for the re-hab quarters.

Imagine the outcome of such a sham socialist enactment: the forcible removal of slum dwellers, the appropriation of land including green areas reserved for the city at large, the forcible introduction of persons not entitled to accommodation into slum rehab buildings; the inflation of free FSI for sale at the top end of market prices, the further densification of the most densely occupied parts of the city and the infliction of further pressure on crumbling utilities, without paying a paisa directly to strengthen the city's infrastructure.

One wonders at the audacity of such shameless and rapacious city governance. Ministers, bureaucrats, builders and the municipality have collaborated in this conspiracy to share the spoils of a development process that continues to dispossess volatile city dwellers. The irony is that as they erect their modern edifices in the name of the poor on a murky foundation of land appropriated from the poor and sustained by fraud, these city developers want to live in these very towers! They do not recognize their obligations to repair the much abused infrastructure in their locality, now to be further strained by these new buildings. The two 60-storey towers in the Tardeo slums are the first in a series of perhaps ten more.

Like Marie Antoinette, the new penthouse royalty of the city perhaps feel that if the poor can't have infrastructure, let them at least have skyscrapers.

Can this situation persist? Not likely. Public interest litigation is being planned, as a last shot at bringing some sanity to bear in the city's planning process. Will those twin towers further the divide between the two cities? Perhaps, the twin-towers of Tardeo will mark a turning point for this great city whose energetic poor are humiliated whenever they enter those miniscule living spaces they call their homes.

An Irish proverb says 'It is in the shelter of each other that people live.' Bombay's builders and their rich clients may forget this only at their own peril.

The under, the over, and the middle world

SANDEEP PENDSE

THE films and the print media would have one believe that Mumbai is the crime capital of the country, what with shootouts, gang wars, murders, assassinations, kidnappings for ransom, and bomb blasts as routine daily occurrences all over the city. The television serials – never to lag too far behind the films – would have it that almost every resident of Mumbai knows at least one don or the other, major or minor. On the other hand Mumbai is popularly considered a safe city – safer than most others for the ordinary person – even for women. An overwhelming majority of the residents would admit that they have never encountered a member of the criminal underworld face to face.

The paradox is not too difficult to understand. The media is ruled by whatever is newsworthy, sensational, spectacular, and different from the ordinary everyday experience. The underworld has in the none too distant past provided outrageously colourful, though often frightening, spectacles. Consider a few scenes. A tenement house considered to be the hideout and headquarters of a criminal gang is attacked by alleged members of a rival gang who all wear identical uniforms, not to masquerade as a security force but as a marker of distinct identity. The uniform is quite unlike that of any security force and quite distinctive.

A custodial cell in a prominent police station is attacked with bombs, its walls breached, and a notorious leader of a dreaded criminal gang lodged in a cell is attacked with firearms and swords. He is ultimately killed. A killer in a sailor's uniform shoots a criminal leader at point blank range in a court of law. The criminal is under police custody and surrounded by armed policemen when the killing takes place. The car of an alleged mastermind of a criminal gang – their 'planner' – is overtaken by other vehicles and stopped. Assailants break the windshield and window panes of the allegedly bullet proof car with sledge hammers and pump bullets into the occupants of the vehicle.

The car of a prominent textile mill owner is chased by other cars. At a traffic signal it is boxed in by the pursuing vehicles and the mill owner shot dead. Yet another mill owner is coolly called out of his office, taken to a waiting vehicle on the road, and shot dead. The most prominent trade unionist in the city is shot dead right outside his house as he leaves in his vehicle. A notorious gangster is shot in a court of law and crippled for life. The tenement house where yet another notorious gang leader resides is so well fortified with an electric fence and so on that the police have to mount an operation to storm it with special equipment.

A major don is attacked in Bangkok by rival Indian gangsters and critically wounded in an action that reads like some special forces operation from a thriller novel. A don just out of jail actually launches a socio-political organization and for its first demonstration manages to mobilize nearly 50,000 people. The gangs are run in the fashion of transnational corporations by CEOs located far away from India, reportedly based in Nepal, Pakistan, UAE, Europe, or even in international waters off the coast of Malaysia.

If these incidents are not enough take the hyperbolic statements attached to the gangsters. Political leaders talk of 'their' dons and 'our' dons. The dons have also been described as 'Hindu' dons – in the same vein as the 'Hindu bomb'. Stunningly, one of them was also described as a 'patriotic don'. To top it all, authoritative sources within the intelligence agencies admitted to the media (after the Bangkok shoot out mentioned above) that if some of the gangs cooperated with the Pakistan intelligence agency, ISI, their rivals cooperated and acted along with the Indian intelligence agency! The alleged involvement of the underworld with the film industry and notable personalities from films lends it even greater glamour.

This indeed is heady stuff for the media. What more can you expect in terms of colour or spectacle than these gems from real life? The films and television serials have in fact rarely portrayed a drama as fantastic or gaudy as this. Even the most successful of them have only depicted in a slightly altered fashion real life characters and incidents.

The common person on the other hand has no reason to ever come across the underworld except through newspaper columns or television news. He only encounters petty crimes. Organized crime – the underworld – has no real or direct involvement in these. It may at best provide some patronage and protection and solve jurisdictional problems. That is precisely why organized crime does not evoke immediate personal anxiety or fear as far as the ordinary residents of the city are concerned.

The only activities of the underworld that they may witness are the so called victimless crimes concerning illicit liquor and illegal gambling. These, to the ordinary residents of the city, particularly those who belong to the working class and related strata, are only technical infringements of the law and not major moral issues. The activities of the underworld and their victims are too far removed from the life world of these people to produce strong reactions. Local lieutenants of the dons may collect protection money from retail shopkeepers. It was once reported that in a bid to extend the net (or expand the market in a manner of speaking) they collected a 'tax' or levy from anyone who bought a car. Such charges on property are again not considered illegitimate by the toiling masses. The underworld figures, in fact, filled the vacuum left by the official social security and welfare apparatus. The dons then had a Robin Hood image.

The underworld – at least a section of it – became infamous and dreaded when it was implicated in the serial bomb blasts of March 1993. The occasional bomb blasts thereafter have been the handiwork of extremist and terrorist elements, not generally of the underworld. That one catastrophic day was enough to change the image. There was of course the genuine anger and fear at the sudden delivery of indiscriminately meted out death. The act also evoked strong nationalist and communal feelings. In fact the media, political commentators and even spokespersons of security agencies if not the government ensured that the communal and nationalist elements remained prominently etched in memory.

The operations of the underworld are romantic and glamorous only in film and television portrayals. The violence in reality is brutal, not justifiable on any grounds. The sole purpose of the crime and violence is making money – more money than honest labour can provide, from rather nefarious activities. The element of social banditry is more found, if at all, in localized smaller gangs than in the activities of the organized criminal underworld which has never displayed any social consciousness even out of a distorted sense of social justice. The 'good deeds' of the criminals were never anything other than marginal acts of charity, comparable to the distribution of alms by 'pious' traders and other varieties of business persons outside any major temple in the city. The apparent popularity some of the gang leaders enjoyed (and there are instances of funerals of slain gang lords attracting crowds in thousands) was based on the employment generation function the underworld performed in some areas of the city, particularly in periods when jobs and occupations were disappearing in the overworld. In its organized form the underworld is an economic operation and to a lesser extent an administrative set-up.

The evolution of the underworld in Mumbai will illustrate the point much better. The underworld is characterized by its organization. Some people allege that petty crime and criminals – including pickpockets, chain snatchers, thefts, housebreaking, robberies – are all organized in Mumbai and under some kind of central control. It is likely that some of the criminals, particularly robbers may team up and function as more or less well-knit groups. However, the grand organization and control of all crime seems to be a fanciful idea. Crime reporters and police officers certainly do not support this notion. (The suspicion of grand organization extends in popular fancy to many activities, including ticketless travel on local trains.)

The roots of gang organization can be traced back many decades. Interestingly, in the earliest phase the organization was connected with industrial labour and political activity. Gangs of determined persons, usually from specific gymnasia in the city, were often employed by employers and anti-strike 'official or recognized' unions to protect strike breakers as they entered the mills, defying pickets to criminally intimidate strikers, disrupt meetings of strike leaders, and assault activists and leaders of the striking workers. Traditionally, such activity was most common in the textile industry since the strikes here were usually industry-wide and carried serious social and political implications. The stakes hence were the highest.

Employment of criminals to intimidate belligerent unions and unionists was not unknown in other industrial establishments either. This had to necessarily be an organized activity given the required numbers and the needed coordination of toughies. Some of the leaders of such gymnasia-based gangs later became recognized political activists and at times even occupied elected posts at the local level. The maintenance of 'troops', forever in readiness and professionally devoted to these activities, itself gave these groups a criminal character – whether or not they were involved in any other infringement of the law. There is enough evidence to suggest that they were involved at least in extortion and collection of 'protection money' from business persons of all varieties. The link of crime with industry and politics thus seem to exist ever since crime got organized. The criminalization of politics and politicization of crime is not a phenomenon only of the recent decades as popularly trumpeted.

The policy of prohibition – a total ban on all manufacture and sale of alcoholic liquor/beverages including even palm wine – is credited by most observers including police officers with the true organization of crime in the city. The criminal activity now acquired structures of production, of transport, of 'wholesale' and 'retail' trade. It now needed many more workers at every stage of operation. It also required equipment for manufacture and transport as well as stable outlets. Obviously this needed investment, patronage and protection. This created the basic organization of criminal activity on an unprecedented scale. Illicit gambling, particularly the numbers rackets, too was organized in a similar fashion; a centrally controlled citywide and statewide organized activity. Territorial disputes, their resolution, implementation of decisions along with enforcement of financial discipline introduced a violent element into these crimes. The criminal gangs now owned and controlled the means of organized violence, useful in industrial disputes, show of political strength and even for electoral manipulation.

Gold has always been a cherished commodity in the country. Its international price was usually lower than the domestic price while the price of silver showed a reverse trend. The restrictions on official import and export of these commodities created an ideal environment for contraband trade – smuggling. The smuggling of gold became intense during the years of 'gold control'. The operation required greater organizational sophistication than that involved in the illicit liquor 'trade' or the numbers rackets. Higher levels of investment, more sophisticated equipment for cross-border (often maritime) as well as intra-country transport and international contacts – all became necessary.

The smugglers obviously could not sell gold in the form it was smuggled in to the ordinary consumer. Consequently links were forged between the underworld and the overworld that are not difficult to imagine. The international dimension and the high stakes further augmented the apparatus of violence; the equipment alone had to match the arsenals of international security and criminal agencies. The 'installed' capacity for violence was often 'spare' and thus could be 'leased' to others who required it. After all, smuggling was not confined to gold. Other commodities too were smuggled, including currency.

Illicit liquor, numbers rackets, and smuggling created 'employment opportunities' for numerous 'workers' at different levels of operations carrying varying degrees of personal risk. In distribution specifically, large numbers were involved. This probably lent a 'social' character to organized crime in the decades of the '70s and '80s. The character was always dual – as strike breakers the criminal gangs directly assaulted the toilers, acting as discipline and peace enforcers in situations where the official security agencies could not. They also created innumerable victims in the toiling masses through liquor, gambling and associated loan sharking, ruining numerous lives.

On the other hand the colourful gang leaders provided employment, some social welfare, some guarantees of security, and an instant as well as transparent if brutal mechanism for solution of disputes and delivery of justice. They also provided illusions of a thrilling, colourful, high-spending lifestyle outside the pale of law and routine concepts of morality.

It will be clear from the above description that the activities and organization of the underworld had some connections with the happenings in the legitimate world. The economic and social happenings as well as particular policies shaped the agenda of the underworld. The easing of the policy of prohibition and liberalization of imports, for example, rendered criminal activities such as bootlegging and smuggling irrelevant or marginal. The narcotics trade for some time attracted the underworld. For various reasons it did not become a major activity though some smuggling of banned substances, including 'industrial' manufactured narcotics, continues to date. The probable ease of alternate routes of transport perhaps never made India a major centre in the narcotics web.

The sphere of organized crime – the underworld – exhibits flexibility in choice of operations and activities that should be the envy of any astute business person. It abandons enterprises as soon as they become irrelevant and then picks up new ones just as possibilities emerge on the horizon. Real estate and construction is one area that has remained fairly common for a long time. This also has a lot to do with the paucity of space and high price of real estate in the city of Mumbai as well as with the nature of the construction industry.

Eviction of tenants from old buildings, repossession of flats for owners, eviction of squatters from plots of land invariably takes a long time if pursued via proper channels in the proper legal forums. The criminals, petty and organized, specialize in 'vacation and repossession' of properties. Single flats probably invite local toughs while entire buildings or blocks of buildings attract larger gangs.

Real estate in Mumbai is also officially highly undervalued. This means that large amounts of black money are involved in the deals – whether that be just the sale or purchase of tenancy rights (not legally permissible) or of large plots of land or the actual construction of buildings and sale of flats. All black money dealings involve risks, particularly that one of the parties may renege or default on payments. There is no legal redress for this grievance. The legal machinery moreover can punish the defaulter but may not be able to recover the money. The underworld in such situations performs the role of the enforcer.

In periods when the construction activity shows signs of boom, the interest rates on loans for the purpose rise. The collection of the principal and interest is generally entrusted to the underworld in case of disputes. This inside knowledge of the construction industry has also taught the underworld that builders are a prime target for extortion and can pay hefty sums for 'protection'. Those who refuse are made examples of through 'elimination'. Their one option is probably to seek police protection. This, however, entails disclosure of the nature and cause of the threat leading to unwelcome attention from other wings of the government machinery. A businessman who receives a threat consequently either prefers to settle the matter by paying the tribute or seeks protection from a rival gangster. Numerous assaults and killings in the city are related to the extortion/protection racket. It is also interesting that top police officials have repeatedly complained that the victims of extortion do not cooperate with the police!

The black money dealings are equally a feature of a number of otherwise legitimate business activity, definitely of most speculative activities. The underworld again plays the role of protector, enforcer, and/or collector in such deals. The larger the deal and more prominent the businessman involved, the bigger the gangster. Recent actions by the police have revealed numerous linkages between legitimate business persons and the underworld. At the root of the links are financial deals.

The film industry attracts attention not only through its glamour but also from the peculiar nature of its financial dealings. It has become a target for various types of extortion. Again, the film trade is an activity where institutionalization particularly in financial matters is weak, the component of black money high and the nature of many deals dubious. Unsurprisingly it creates space for enforcers and collectors who may then overstep their brief and begin to operate for own interest and gain.

A few marginal notes are needed to conclude this cursory survey. The nature of crime and of criminal organization has changed. The logic of contemporary capitalism does not leave even the world of crime alone. The underworld too by all accounts acquires a corporate structure and logic. It becomes impersonal and professional. The violence becomes clinical, to be used as a means almost without passion.

There is already a strange dispersal and yet centralization in terms of control of the underworld. The reigning dons and their most valued lieutenants are outside India. Rather, secondary and transitory 'under-bosses' control and execute the operations in the city, but according to a central plan. The shooters are new recruits who know nothing about the key operations, key operatives or even the dimensions of the particular operation they are involved in. They are primarily ancillaries or independent functionaries contracted for particular activity with a full element of deniability and of loss of connecting threads.

The activity and modus operandi change rapidly. The underworld becomes transnationalized and yet it operates through stand-alone subsidiaries that will not produce any domino effect in their fall, should one occur. The underworld in a way mimics the global corporation – it becomes as predatory, as penetrating, and yet as invisible. This very global corporate character also takes away the individual machismo, the social bandit sentiment, the search for justice.

The dons of the Mumbai underworld are different from the daredevil desperados in some other areas of the country. The underworld no longer has a home country, no metropolis that it is inseparably tied to. Like speculative capital it shifts areas of operation. Reversals or even bankruptcies in one place do not mean a total global collapse. The firm merely cuts losses and shifts its area of operation.

The transnational nature of the operations brings the underworld in contact with intelligence agencies. The underworld represents the perfect private agency for state sponsored terrorist activities in another country. The 'spare' capacity for transporting contraband for mindless violence, for intimidation or terrorization, is leased out or subcontracted to the highest bidder. The payment need not always be in hard cash. It can be in safe havens, in studied ignorance of certain activities, in information, in equipment, in protection. The fanatic elements in the terrorist networks can be ably supplemented by the apolitical professional operatives of the crime corporation. It should be no surprise at all to have two more clients with diametrically opposed motives and goals. It would still fulfil the contracts with almost no conflict of interest.

The ground reality may be more complicated. It involves the working of social pressures that local subsidiaries are subject to as well as the local links they have to build for sheer survival. It is true worldwide that marginalized communities and ethnic groups provide the human power – usually the cannon fodder and sometimes even the leadership of the organized criminal underworld. The same situation exists in India and in Mumbai. Planned economic ruination like the one attempted in Gujarat recently, combined with the anger and disillusionment with the rule of law such pogroms evoke, provides foot soldiers in even larger numbers for the criminal and the disruptive and/or terrorist activities.

The 'nexus' between criminals – particularly organized crime, the underworld – and the police force as well as the politicians has repeatedly featured in discussions. There is of course the element of corruption as far as connections with the police force are concerned. There are other considerations too. It would seem that there is an implicit (rabbit garden) law enforcement policy that 'tolerates' certain levels and types of crime.

This is at one level a pragmatic measure. A city of 12 million cannot be effectively policed by less than 50,000 law enforcement officers. Not every crime can be prevented, detected, prosecuted or punished. Some kinds of priorities have to be set. Moreover, officially too some connections have to be maintained to gather information and intelligence. Additionally the policy at the higher level is to go easy on certain gangs at certain times. The reasons for this are various. It now seems that some gangsters are used as unofficial intelligence assets. It would be naïve to expect that there are no contacts whatsoever between the underworld and law enforcement agencies anywhere in the world.

The relationship between the political sphere and the underworld, by no means recent, is a more complex issue. It has perhaps become more overt now. Again corruption is definitely one factor in the relationship, as is illegal services sought and rendered. In the days when crime had a social banditry component to it, the contacts and connections were natural and unavoidable. The gangsters then also enjoyed social backing and social bases with a capacity to mobilize the masses. This made contacts, cooperative or adversarial, inevitable.

Subsequently, the criminals lost the social banditry element and certain political organizations made systematic intimidation and terrorization of both supporters and opponents their permanent method and style of operation. This introduced systematic use of violence, sometimes against specific political trends and sometimes against specific sections of people. The dependence on criminal gangs for weapons and perpetrators of professional violence became common.

Such organizations openly patronized particular gangs and gangsters, at times awarding them peculiar sobriquets – the son of the soil gangster, the Hindu don, the patriotic don, and so on. This is a deterioration of politics itself – the nexus with criminals is only a part of this alteration. When political policies include pogroms, dependence on professional perpetrators of brutal inhumanity becomes necessary. Strangely the denunciation has been only of individual corrupt contacts not of the systematic relationships.

This is perhaps not very surprising. The fear and apparent or feigned revulsion that the criminal underworld evokes is because of its overt use of violence. A Big Bull scamster perhaps harmed the economy far more and ruined more lives and institutions only a few years ago. Till incarceration he was lionised by the 'overworld' even after the details of his crimes became public. He graced many a publication with columns as also business schools as guest faculty. He also addressed numerous chaste and respectable gatherings. His world was never considered to be the 'underworld'. It was perhaps too close to the elite 'overworld'.

Big business and entrepreneurship

GITA PIRAMAL

IN any study of entrepreneurship, should success be measured by longevity or resilience?[1] One way to answer this question is to see how Mumbai's leading business families have coped with upheavals between 1964 and 1999. Let's start by looking at the top 50 business houses of India from 1964 to 1999, and then drill down to the Mumbai groups in that list (see Tables I and II). What are the key findings?

Size matters: Bigger family groups either take longer to wither away or are more resilient. Mumbai's shooting stars of the 1964-90, i.e., groups which dropped out of the ranking (Mangaldas Parekh, Scindia, Vissanji, Thackersey and Kilachand) are all from the bottom half of the list. Similarly, business families which dropped out of the list between 1990-99 (Chowgule, Mehra, Ghia, Ashok Birla and Nirlon) are also from the bottom half of the list. It should be noted however that Godrej drops out because a substantial part of the

1. Longevity does imply a continuous ability to cope with change. Here a subtle implication is being suggested: resilience here refers to the ability to weather sudden, abrupt, life threatening change. Longevity is the marathon, resilience the sprint.

group is privately held. On the other hand, though the performance of groups like Walchand, Kirloskar and Khatau (who were in the top half) was clearly sliding, they took longer to drop out of the list.

The list of survivors in this 35-year-period is equally interesting: five of Mumbai's business groups (Tata, Birla, Bajaj, Mahindra and Wadia) appear to have taken the huge changes in the competitive environment in their stride with remarkable dexterity. J.R.D. Tata was group chairman in 1939, Ratan Tata, his nephew, heads it today. G.D. Birla's great-grandson, Kumar Mangalam, presides over India's sixth biggest business group. Nusli Wadia grafted a petrochemical-to-biscuits business on the textile inheritance created by Sir Ness Wadia while Anand Mahindra and Rahul Bajaj are expanding on the base inherited from their grandfathers.

Taking the entire sample, the activity at the lower end of the two tables is more hectic than at the top as new groups thrust upwards. The large number of new groups in the 1990-99 period could also be because of the change in calculation from assets to market capitalization.

Family splits effect: Of the drop outs among Mumbai business houses between 1964-99, there have been family divorces in almost half the business groups: Thackersey, Kilachand, Ghia, Walchand, Khatau. Would they, could they, have remained in the top 50 league had they stayed together? It's a moot point. Table II also shows splintered Mumbai groups: Aditya Birla, Ajay Piramal, Harsh Mariwala, Rajen Raheja and Vijaypat Singhania. Would they, could they, have made it to the table had they not split up?

Focus and diversification: One key change taking place – today's family groups are more likely to be running one large company while the earlier business houses were diversified conglomerates. For example, in the 1964 list, we see that almost every group has a finger in several pies. Kilachand and Khatau were perhaps the least diversified, in the sense that though they had large financial interests in several companies, the family managed only a few companies, largely in cotton textiles. Bajaj in 1964 was a fairly diversified group:

work on launching Bajaj Auto had begun. Mukund Steel (a joint venture with Viren Shah) was up and running, the sugar mill which was the basis of their industrial activities was humming away as were numerous smaller concerns.

The 1999 list however is radically different. Leaving aside the Tatas and the Birlas, the 1999 list presents a completely different picture with as many as seven of the new Mumbai groups being tightly focused on one business, and very often operating though just one company.

This move away from diversification and conglomerates can partly – but not wholly – be explained by changes in government legislation. Earlier, markets were small and highly entrepreneurial businessmen would enter another market as growth flattened in a particular business or segment. In the 1960s and later, the main routes open for groups hungry for growth were acquisitions or growth outside India. There were limits to organic growth and entrepreneurship with government restrictions on size straitjacketing business families, forcing them to diversify into unrelated business.

In 1991, many of the draconian provisions of the MRTP Act were discarded releasing a surge of energy. More important perhaps was the Dhirubhai Ambani factor. The size and scale of the Patalganga, Hazira and Jamnagar complexes encouraged Indian business families – and Indian bureaucrats and politicians – to shed their 'small is beautiful' mindset. Financial results were another factor and the visible success of companies such as Bajaj Auto who refused to diversify was not lost. Difficulties in managing several companies in different businesses in an increasingly complex environment became another reason for groups to stay focused. By 1999, only 18 family groups were conglomerates. And even out of these 18, for many groups such as Ambani, Bajaj, Wadia and Mahindra, their market cap was dominated by one flagship company. Core competency became the new buzzword and 31 of the new family groups appear to swear by it.

Another reason could be the change in calculation. It is no secret that fund managers prefer to invest in focused companies –

they prefer their portfolio to be diversified than the companies they invest in, thereby pushing up the market cap of companies which are focused and downgrading companies which are in several businesses. Indian business families are reacting to this change by restructuring their holdings. The Aditya Birla group headed by Kumar Mangalam, for example, is merging its cement interests into one large company instead of being divisions in half a dozen firms.

However, it should also be noted that of the 31 family groups which dropped out of the Top 50 between 1990-99, quite a few were in fact focused in their particular areas, such as the Singhanias of LML, the Mehras of Orkay, the Seths of Garden Silk, and the Shroffs of Facor, to name just a few.

Quality of management: The composition of the family groups in the two tables suggest that external factors are important but internal issues are perhaps more important. After independence, Indian family groups indulged in furious asset-building and created several mega-empires. As we have seen, a few survived but most crumbled into the ashes of rusting plant and machinery. An inability to withstand the zephyrs of change, outdated technology, outright mismanagement, over-stretched resources, poor labour-management skills – the reasons for failure are myriad.

A comparison between Scindia and Inchcape may be in order. Both Scindia and Inchcape have dropped out of the lists. Scindia Steamship used to be Indian entrepreneurship's proudest achievement. From the moment of its birth, it faced the hostility of the world's biggest shipping firm, the British India Steamship Corporation (otherwise known as the BI) and its doughty chairman, Lord Inchcape. Inchcape used every trick in the trade to try and destroy Scindia but failed. From a single liner firm in 1919, Scindia became India's flagship carrier in 1947 and was a Top 20 company until well into the sixties. Or until its gerontocratic management achieved what Inchcape could not. By the 1990s, it had sunk without a trace. The Inchape group wound up its affairs in India at the end of the Raj and continues to function in the UK.

Table I

Top 50 Business Groups 1964-99

	1964 *GROUP*	*Assets*	*1990* *GROUP*	*Assets*	*1999* *GROUP*	*Mkt C*
1	Tata (incl ACC)*	369.11	Tata (excl ACC)*	7546	Tata (excl ACC)*	22345
2	Birla	290.24	Birla	7235	Premji (Wipro)	18439
3	Martin Burn	108.72	Ambani*	3241	Ambani*	16060
4	Thapar	70.61	JK Singhania	1829	Singh (Ranbaxy)	7970
5	Bangur	65.29	Thapar	1763	Bajaj*	7667
6	Sahu Jain	61.06	Mafatlal*	1297	Aditya V Birla*	7204
7	Shriram	59.85	Bajaj*	1228	Munjal (Hero)	3715
8	Bird Heilgers	58.29	Modi	1192	Mohan (Punjab Tractors)	3173
9	JK Singhania	54.43	MA Chidambaram	1032	Raju (Satyam computers)	–
10	Sarabhai	54.29	TVS	909	Wadia*	2985
11	Walchand*	54.02	Shriram	800	Mahindra*	2910
12	Surajmal Nagarmal	44.83	UB	716	Hamied (Cipla)	2824
13	Goenka	43.56	Bangur	674	Pentafour	2742
14	Mafatlal*	43.11	Kirloskar*	633	Dr. Reddy's	2723
15	Andrew Yule	34.30	Walchand*	626	Sekhsaria (Guj Ambuja Cement)*	2719
16	Apte Amalgamations	33.43	Mahindra*	620	Subhash Chandra*	2258
17	Jardine Henderson	31.42	Goenka	570	TVS	1986
18	Bajaj*	29.25	Nanda (Escorts)	537	Vinay Rai (Usha Rectifiers)	1876
19	BIC	29.05	Lalbhai	479	Burman (Dabur)	1859
20	Macneill & Barry	26.98	Ruia (Essar)*	437	Khorakhiwala (Wockhardt)*	1315
21	Lalbhai	26.20	Garware*	437	Anil Agarwal (Sterlite)	–
22	Binny	25.40	Sarabhai	384	Ruia (Essar)*	1278
23	Killick	24.45	Wadia*	366	Ajay Piramal*	1261
24	Rallis	24.45	Khaitan	354	Nambiar (BPL)	1225
25	Kilachand*	24.30	Bhiwandiwala	345	Patel (Nirma)	1159
26	Swedish Match	23.92	Chowgule*	335	MS Oberoi	1135
27	TVS	23.33	Godrej*	331	Asian Paints*	1032
28	Balmer Lawrie	21.68	Khatau*	329	Hinduja	969
29	GD Kothari	21.55	Singhania (Lohia)	326	Harsh Mariwala (Marico)*	–
30	Kirloskar*	21.46	MS Oberoi	301	India Cement	886
31	A&F Harvey	21.14	Mehra (Orkay)*	267	Rajan Raheja*	880

contd...

...contd...

	1964 GROUP	Assets	1990 GROUP	Assets	1999 GROUP	Mkt C
32	Mahindra*	21.11	Raunaq Singh	247	Chhabria (Finolex)	879
33	Modi	20.82	Seth (Garden Silk)	245	Khaitan	879
34	Scindia*	20.62	Raasi Cement	243	Square D	874
35	Vissanji*	20.62	V Ramkrishna	233	Mapillai (MRF)	822
36	BN Elias	20.44	Muruggapa	230	Thapar	798
37	Turner Morrison	19.25	Sahu Jain	230	Sun Pharma	794
38	Jai Dayal Dalmia	19.07	R Mody (Hind Dev)	223	RP Goenka	740
39	Parry	18.91	GV Naidu	217	Jindal	647
40	Wadia*	18.09	Ghia*	211	Sheth (GE Ship)*	642
41	Thiagaraja	17.96	Mapillai (MRF)	201	KK Birla	618
42	Jaipuria	17.78	Apeejay	193	Murugappa	612
43	Ruia	17.20	Ashok Birla*	191	Vijaypat Singhania*	611
44	Bhagirath Kanoria	16.78	Dalmia (GTC)	180	Kalyani	598
45	GV Naidu	16.05	Nirlon*	174	Torrent	590
46	Thackersey*	15.00	India Cement	167	Dhoot (Videocon)*	573
47	Khatau*	14.23	Shri Ambica	164	Parekh (Pidilite)*	572
48	Mangaldas Parekh*	13.90	Shroff (Facor)	145	Balaji (Reddy)	572
49	Amin	13.31	Parry	140	Adani	551
50	Seshasayee	13.22	Kothari	138	UB	543

Source: Compiled from Monopoly Inquiry Report 1964-65, 75 Largest Business Groups in Indian Private Corporate Sector; The MRTP Commission, *The Economic Times*, 5 August 1991; CMIE and company reports for 1999. * – Mumbai Business Houses.

The dropouts are broadly of two types: (*i*) Older groups who founded or acquired their businesses in the 1950s and 1960s such as Mafatlal, Shriram, Kirloskar, Walchand, Lalbhai, Khatau, Sahu Jain, G.V. Naidu, and Parry. (*ii*) Newer groups which were active in the 1980s such as the Delhi-based, highly diversified Modi group; Deepak Singhania of LML; the Mumbai-based Mehra brothers of Orkay; Praful Seth of Garden Silk Mills with his state-of-the-art design room which forced Indian mills to upgrade textile design; Virenchee Sagar and Manhar Bhagat of Nirlon; and the Shroffs of Facor.

Both sets of groups faced very different challenges. In the second cluster, in several cases, new entrepreneurs challenged them in their businesses with larger and better run facilities. In the first cluster, internal managerial issues seem to be the bigger challenges.

Sometimes, as in the case of the Mafatlal group, both factors came to play with disastrous effect. The group was founded by Mafatlal Gagalbhai (1873-44) when he acquired a small defunct mill in Ahmedabad in 1905. By 1930, the group was running nine mills, and had a pie in insurance, retail, financial services, textile trading and for brief moments, a jute mill and a shipping company. The group's most ambitious foray however was in petrochemicals and in 1963 it pioneered Nocil, a project large enough for *Time* magazine to fly a reporter from New York to Bombay. By the 1990s however, low investments in technology and the growth of the powerloom sector had sapped the Mafatlal group's textile business. Nocil became a pygmy in front of the Ambani's Reliance group. And internecine family dynamics contributed further to the group's decline.

Industry sector: So is success simply a question of being in the right business at the right time, as the cliché goes? Maybe so. In the 1930s, businesses which did well were cotton textiles, jute, sugar, cement, shipping, engineering, and tea. By the 1960s, the horizons had expanded and families engaged in paper, cotton textiles, construction, pharmaceuticals, and chemicals started doing well. In the 1990s, favourite sectors appear to be IT, petrochemicals, pharmaceuticals, two wheelers, jeeps and tractors, biscuits, cement, and electronic entertainment.

The brown (*burra*) sahebs: In some cases the family has disappeared, but the company has survived through a change in management. In the post-independence period we therefore see the rise of the brown burra sahebs. These families presided over the disintegration of the British commercial raj. In 1939, 32 of the leading 50 managing agency firms were owned by the British. After independence, the British gradually withdrew their capital out of these firms and the brown sahebs acquired the giant orphans and nursed them to health – sometimes.

Thus B.M. Khaitan acquired MacLeod and Williamson to cobble together a group which by the 1990s controlled almost 5% of the world tea market. The Goenkas acquired the Armenian-

Table II

Mumbai Business Groups

Rank	1964 *GROUP*	*Assets*	*Rank*	1990 *GROUP*	*Assets*	*Rank*	1999 *GROUP*	*Mkt C*
1	Tata (incl ACC)	369.11	1	Tata (excl ACC)	7546	1	Tata (excl ACC)	22345
11	Walchand	54.02	3	Ambani	3241	3	Ambani	16060
14	Mafatlal	43.11	6	Mafatlal	1297	5	Bajaj	7667
18	Bajaj	29.25	7	Bajaj	1228	6	Aditya V Birla	7204
25	Kilachand	24.30	14	Kirloskar	633	10	Wadia	2985
30	Kirloskar	21.46	15	Walchand	626	11	Mahindra	2910
32	Mahindra	21.11	16	Mahindra	620	15	Sekhsaria (Guj Ambuja Cement)	2719
34	Scindia	20.62	20	Ruia (Essar)	437	16	Subhash Chandra	2258
35	Vissanji	20.62	21	Garware	437	20	Khorakhiwala (Wockhardt)	1315
40	Wadia	18.09	23	Wadia	366	22	Ruia (Essar)	1278
46	Thackersey	15.00	26	Chowgule	335	23	Ajay Piramal	1261
47	Khatau	14.23	27	Godrej	331	27	Asian Paints	1032
48	Mangaldas Parekh	13.90	28	Khatau	329	29	Harsh Mariwala (Marico)	–
			31	Mehra (Orkay)	267	31	Rajan Raheja	880
			40	Ghia	211	40	Sheth (GE Ship)	642
			41	Ashok Birla	191	43	Vijaypat Singhania	611
			42	Nirlon	174	46	Dhoot (Videocon)	573
							Parekh (Pidilite)	572

owned Duncan Brothers in the 1960s. The family split in the late 1970s, leading to the birth of RPG Enterprises. In 1999, Spencer and Harrisons contributed to RPG Enterprises's Rs 740 million market cap. Meanwhile the takeover tycoon of the 1980s, Manu R. Chhabria, acquired rich old groups of the 1930s such as Dunlop, Shaw Wallace. Finlay became Tata Tea which passed from Leslie Sawhney (JRD's brother-in-law) to Darbari Seth for nurturing while Freddie Mehta was asked to look after Forbes and Nani Palkhivala headed ACC. Parry was taken over by the Murugappa Group.

The private sector seems to have done a better job than the government which tried to resuscitate the tattered elements of former British groups such as Martin Burn and Andrew Yule with limited success.

Geography: Curiously the biggest survivors – Tata and Birla – are based in western India. Any pre-1947 analysis would typically be heavily tilted in favour of Kolkata (the big British groups) and Mumbai (a miscellaneous collection of textile dynasties). However, by the 1960s, southern and northern groups have begun to make their presence felt and by 1999 there is a much more rounded, all-India character.

This quick look raises some interesting questions. The 1960s saw Kolkata's jute groups tumbling. The 1970s saw a decimation of the Gujarati textile aristocracy in Mumbai and Ahmedabad. The 1980s saw a surprising erosion of the northern groups. The 1990s have seen the upsurge of the IT sector and pharma-based groups.

Equally, in the period 1990-91, no new family group emerged from eastern India. There are 18 family groups from western India (Premji here has been clubbed in the western India group as he started out in Mumbai though the group's headquarters are now in Bangalore). The north has contributed nine new groups while five have come from the south. Ironically, if 18 new business family groups from western India made their mark in 1990-91, 16 groups from western India dropped out.

Community: In his 1977 study on the effects of industrial licensing, Ravi K. Hazari, a leading economist and bureaucrat, had pointed out that the Marwaris were India's most aggressive business community. By 1999, while their dominance continued, the clout has begun to fade. The family groups in the 1999 list come from varied communities, several of which are not traditionally commercial ones. Some of the obvious trends include the dropping out of Maharashtrian groups such as Kirloskar, Garware and Walchand from the 1999 list, as well as the entry of Muslim groups such as Premji, Hamied and Khorakhiwala.

At the same time, the relevance of business communities today has diminished to virtually zero. In an era when information trickled in slowly, community networks were a source of competitive advantage. The community, with its unique referral system, was also a helpful way of hiring managers when head-hunting was unheard of. The network also provided seed capital at a pinch. These were important and tangible benefits but by the 1990s and 2000s, most of these functions had been taken over by other institutions and entrepreneurs no longer need to rely on their membership to a business community for financial and managerial aid.

Some notes on the data

Why 1964 and not 1947? The year 1964 is a turning point because this was when the Monopolies and Restrictive Trade Practices Commission was established. By that year, the MRTP Commission had finished collecting and sifting information on Indian big business and hence reliable data is available. (See Table I: Family Business Groups 1964-99). The next interesting turning point is 1991, when the P.V. Narasimha Rao administration introduced the New Economic Policy, hence MRTP Commission data for March 1990 is used. The advantage lies in that it permits comparison between 1964 and 1990 given that data for both years is based on a common platform.

Strictly speaking the data for 1990 and 1999 is not comparable. The 1990 data uses assets as the basis for ranking the top 50 business families of India while the figures for 1999 are based on market capitalization. One could have calculated market cap for the top 50 groups in 1990 or their assets for 1999. However, by taking the popular yardstick of the time, the comparison yields some interesting trends. Using these three types of data also helps somewhat in measuring the effect of change.

The beginnings of the art movement*

KEKOO GANDHY

AMONG the European painters who came to India during the War was Walter Langhammer, an Austrian. He was a contemporary of the famous painter Oskar Kokoschka, who was professor of the Academy in Vienna in the 1930s. There was this Parsi girl called Silloo Vakil from Bombay who was studying with him and she used to say to him, 'Walter, you must come to India one day,' and he would say 'Ja, ja.' So when Hitler came along and he had to leave Austria, he wrote to Vakil, saying that he would like to come to India. And she walked into the office of Sir Francis Low, editor of *The Times of India*, and said, 'I am the daughter of Rotarian Vakil and I would like you to promise me something.' She was cheeky enough to do that. The result was that Langhammer was appointed as the first art director of the TOI. The year must have been 1936. And at the time it had the only colour annual number.

Langhammer fell in love with the light and colour of India and all the young artists. Here, he would often say, he saw a future in the

---

* As told to grand-daughter, Anisha Imhasly.

modern art movement – he felt it was all over Europe. So people like Ara, Raza, Hussain, Souza and Raiba, the great names of the Indian Progressive Art Movement, became his students. Every Sunday, it was open house at his studio on Nepean Sea Road.

He would tell them what makes a good painting. He would share his experiences of Europe and tell them about events in the art world, seen at first hand. They found a windfall in this readymade teacher. And he had so much love and affection for them. It was not just the artists alone – the people around them too were responsible, in a way, for the birth of the Progressives. There were factors like the excitement over the prospect of impending Independence, the feeling that now Indian artists would not have to go through Westminster, that India would have its own embassies in different parts of the world, and that we would be able to make our own connections.

Remember that in those days, Indian artists had no means of going abroad or of following trends in Europe. Of course, there were magazines, but the unexpected arrival of all these Europeans – most of them Jews fleeing from Austria – really started the Progressive movement off. Apart from Langhammer, there was Dr. E. Schlesinger and Rudi von Leyden, both German. Rudi was the chief PRO of Volkart Brothers, a Swiss trading company based in India, and he had a younger brother, A.R. Leyden, a sculptor who styled himself as a painter after Langhammer and was called 'little Langhammer'. They had arrived before Langhammer because their father foresaw the arrival of Hitler by two or three years. They were all warm and outgoing people, generous too. The founder chairman of Larsen and Toubro, a Danish gentleman called Holck Larsen, was one of the earliest art patrons. They were also the 'in people' of the time. They were written about in the papers very often.

With Langhammer came a lot of professionals, doctors… a sort of mini-influx of Jews. They valued art and provided patronage. Schlesinger was so attached to Mohan Samant, one of the Progressive artists, that he would travel by local train to Goregaon to see what he was up to. They had a great enthusiasm for Indian artists – who else was interested? – and they pioneered buying. They were not the only foreigners to influence the new art movement.

Towards the end of the War, with operations ongoing in North Africa, Italian POWs were brought in by the British and domiciled in camps all over India. Captain Dust, an Englishman, decided that these able-bodied men should be put to some work. Among them were car mechanics, painters and waiters. He selected those who could use a brush and formed a separate unit in the army called MURART. The idea was to get them to paint and use their work across all army establishments in South Asia. Dust went to Mountbatten with a proposal and, imaginative as he was, Mountbatten accepted the idea and put him in charge. He was given a building at Chakala near Sahar airport. The POWs were equipped with soft boards and were asked to paint. That is how these Italian men started creating paintings here in Bombay.

Meanwhile, back on vacation from Cambridge (I never went back) during the War, I met a Belgian gentleman who had landed up in India called Van Damme. His father had been a framer and restorer of the great Flemish masters. He had heard a news story back home about the many gods and goddesses that Indians kept in their homes. He knew that India would be a captive market to sell frames. Our acquaintance led to the establishment of the Chemould framing factory in 1940. He gave me know-how, we got the finance together and my brother Rusi and I set up the factory.

Around the time Dust was putting together his idea, the Chemould factory was in a plot behind our bungalow called Shapur Baug in Chakala. The Leela Hotel stands there today. It was a very pretty place with mango and chikoo *wadis*. The British requisitioned the ground floor of this bungalow for MURART. Wood was scarce because it was requisitioned for the war effort. We did not know how to continue with our business. Luckily, MURART said they needed frames for all these paintings they were churning out and they started supplying us with wood. We worked exclusively for them.

For soldiers, the Italians were really good artists. They would come home on Sundays. We handed the kitchen over to them and they would prepare all these risottos. They were lonely people, far from home, so we tried to help them by selling the private work they did, not the ones they made for MURART. Food was rationed at the time, but they were soldiers and had everything. They used to bake lovely cookies. We began to invite over our friends and other Indian artists. Everyone had a good time and after dinner a hat was passed around. For Rs 100 or 200, you could pick up one of the finest paintings of the time and everyone was happy.

Collecting art was really started by a few individuals. Though there was no art movement or recognized artists around, Bombay's first generation of collectors were quite generous. Ratan Tata's father, Naval Tata, was a very kind man. We had a party at his house in Juhu and in one night sold 10 or 12 paintings, some of the private work of the Italians and some by our own Indian painters. Bombay then had the right mix of socialites and patrons. We were, of course, trying to make it a fashion statement, so that people would feel that it was the in thing to buy art. Since there were no galleries then, all this was done at our homes.

Much later, in the early seventies, when Holck Larsen was still chairman of Larsen and Toubro, I remember telling him that Jamshedji Tata believed that by picking out talented people from across the country and nurturing them, he was doing the greatest service to the country. Immediately, he told me to name an artist and he would look after him. So a Bangladeshi refugee called Bhushan was installed at the factory, supplied with materials and told that all he had to do was create art. He stayed for three years.

But coming back to the early forties, one Christmas I was at Porcupine Point in Matheran and I met Schimmel, another Austrian. When he learned that I ran Chemould, he asked me to meet his good friend Langhammer as soon as I got back to Bombay. In those days, we were making mouldings for paintings, but Langhammer asked us to make frames. And he explained to me his vision for Indian art. He really believed that contemporary Indian art would make a mark and have an impact on the art scene in the world. He even compared it in terms of impact to the French Impressionist movement. When he said 'Indian art', he was referring to the various schools – the Bengal school, miniature paintings, the influence of Indian sculpture. India had a great store of inspiration to draw from and the colours and light of India would make the difference, he felt.

Meanwhile, the Progressive artists were working hard to establish their own identity. They were working on a very deliberate policy of establishing their own personalities and not using past traditions to express themselves. At that time, the J.J. School of Art had two sections – Indian and western – with different principals. Jagannath Ahiwasi looked after the Indian section and at the western section was Charles Gerrard, a Jew from England. But the question on everyone's mind was: where do we go from here?

People like Souza and Ara were not sticking to the academic conventions of painting and nor were they students of the Indian section, which concentrated on miniatures. All the encouragement from Langhammer and his circle of art collectors at the Bombay Art Society, a most vibrant and prestigious body, gave them a place of their own. They said, we are what we are. We don't want to copy the West. We are products of our immediate environments and want to establish our identity by being contemporary.

The Bombay Art Society was set up in the latter part of the last century by the masters of academic painting, most of whom were traditional artists from the academies of the West. There, artists were taught to take a canvas, prime it, grind colour and be responsible for the painting right up to the varnishing stage. For the Indian artists who were learning from them, all this was very new. Oil paint was not part of the Indian tradition. The Indians were experts at watercolours on cloth, or murals and frescoes.

This was one of the earliest exchanges between the West and India in art. The society had an annual event, a gold medal for the artist of the year, and without doubt it was the most prestigious art award. Artists before the Progressives like Durdhankar, Haldhankar and Pithawala had won this award. Later, artists like Hussain and Amrita Shergill were also honoured.

Leyden introduced me very enthusiastically to Ara. Ara came from a humble background and I remember Gallery Chemould sponsored his first exhibition at Chetna in the late forties. Rajeswar Rao, the writer, came down from Paris and Mulk Raj Anand was back from London, and we were keen that it should be a big success. I remember inviting people down the road from my home – doctors, dentists, people we knew personally, we told them to go and they bought paintings for Rs 200 or so.

Leyden supported Ara for a long time. When Ara made some money from the exhibition, he wanted to give it to Leyden. But Leyden opened a bank account for him with that money and told him that he was on his own.

I shared a close personal relationship with Hebbar. I first met him at Langhammer's studio and we shared a lot of enthusiasm for the independence of the country. We hero-worshipped Nehru. But after the Chinese conflict we could not possibly go on like that. We remained great friends, despite the fact that our ideologies had changed. He was the one who introduced me to Gerrard, who was then Dean of the School of Art.

Hussain was a favourite of Wayne Hartwell, who was the librarian at the USIS, opposite Khadi Bhandar. You could walk straight into his office off the pavement. This was in 1946 and he was one of the most consummate buyers of our set, as well as a very good friend. He and his wife loved the work of Hussain and Chavda. Don't forget that Husain was a nobody then. He was to rise to great heights later, but at the time it was Chavda who was sought after. He had a powerful personality. Unlike most of the others, he was an educated, sophisticated and quiet person. One of Hussain's paintings, Doll's Wedding, was part of a Chemould exhibition and was picked up by Hartwell. He took it home with him and we heard that it had changed hands. It was finally sold for $35,000 in the mid-eighties and I know Wayne had bought it for Rs 300 in the 1940s right here in Bombay.

I can't say honestly that I was interested in art to begin with, or that I had any great knowledge of it. I got interested through my friends Langhammer and Leyden, after seeing their great enthusiasm for contemporary Indian art. I was moved by their belief in the future of Indian contemporary art. And once I began interacting with the artists – they were such beautiful, trusting people, Ara and Raza and Hebbar – I felt I could be a go-between. As a Rotarian, I was meeting a certain class of people, and I felt I had a distinctive role to play and, in particular, a vested interest in the framing of their art.

I had a vested interest in seeing a picture transformed by a frame, when it would stand a better chance of finding a buyer. Indian art then had no market, and it gave me a lot of satisfaction to be part of a process that sold paintings. There was no commission in those days. Then came a time when artists would leave their paintings – Raza, Palsikar, Ara, Gade, Raiba. Raiba was so badly off that we had to give him a job at the framing factory. But the great thing was that they trusted us.

They would all leave their paintings with us. We had a place called Haroon House next to a stationery mart behind the Reserve Bank. There, we displayed some of the paintings that came to us for framing. The Metro Cinema opened with a lot of fanfare and we took a portion of the wall on the first floor and called it the Metro Art Corner. When people came out after the show, they would see the paintings. And we had a window on the first floor of the Taj from 1944 to 1948. Then we realized that we needed a bigger place, since we were selling a fair number of paintings there. My father had a godown on Princess Street, which we turned into a framing shop. Roshan Kalapesi showed initiative in displaying art and framing all the paintings. The Progressives made their first sales through this shop and the Artists Centre at Rampart Row.

So that became the first regular place for display, where we showed all these paintings that the artists had left behind. Then

Homi Bhabha, who was setting up the Tata Institute of Fundamental Research, came over after lunch and started examining our frames with a great deal of interest. He was very meticulous about framing.

We soon recognized discerning and interested art patrons and started holding private exhibitions. We had previews for Homi Bhabha, which is why the Tata Institute of Fundamental Research (TIFR) has the best private collection of forties art. The contagion spread among our set from Langhammer and Leyden to Homi Bhabha and Farookh Mulla, PRO of the Tatas. They were all patrons of the Chemould shop.

At our first Hussain exhibition, I looked out of the window and saw my wife's uncle, the founder-owner of *Parsiana* magazine, passing by. I just pulled him in and said we needed a crowd. The poor man had no idea what was going on. But Hussain sold so well that we were flooded with work from artists all over India. After that exhibition, our sales of frames and art shot up from Rs 5,000 per year to Rs 20,000 per year. That is when Mulla, Langhammer, Leyden and I got together – Sir Cowasji Jehangir was there too – to discuss how we could handle this sudden growth of interest. The implication was that artists in Bombay needed a gallery. So we put this to Sir Cowasji Jehangir, who was already a patron, and though a political person (he was a crucial mediator between Gandhi and Jinnah and was active in the Legislative Assembly), he also bought art.

He hailed from a long line of visionary benefactors. Two hundred years ago, his great-great grandfather had founded the Bombay University Hall, the next generation gave the city the building where the National Gallery of Modern Art is housed, and the next sponsored Elphinstone College. He granted the funds for setting up the Jehangir Art Gallery in 1951-52. The museum gave the land and they had a tripartite agreement. He had the foresight to put nominees of the Bombay Arts Society on the management committee of the Jehangir Art Gallery; the idea was to differentiate the promotion of art from the sale of art.

We were invited by the committee to set up a gallery on the first floor. We started the Chemould art gallery in 1951. I was persuaded by artists like Souza and Chavda not to do this. They said, 'You will never recover your investments.' Somehow, we did not make losses but our profits from the framing company certainly fell. Since I was already with the Bombay Arts Society set, I was really in the thick of things and with the help and support of my wife Khorshed, we continued to promote art independently as the proprietors of Gallery Chemould.

It has given us great joy to support the art movement and see it grow from strength to strength. Today we continue to support exhibitions like the one my wife put together called 'The Portrait of a Community', which opened at the National Gallery of Modern Art in October 2002. We have both retired from the running of the Gallery Chemould, which our youngest daughter Shireen continues to run, and the framing factory has been taken over by our son Adil.

Unseen, under our noses

SALEEM A. AHMADULLAH

BOMBAY is justifiably renowned for its Indo-Saracenic and Gothic architecture. The older part of South Mumbai, as Bombay is now called, has many magnificent buildings constructed in the second half of the 19th century and the first quarter of the 20th. These impressive buildings must have made the main 'visual' argument for Bombay to be designated the '*urbs prima in Indis*'. They have been the subject of countless photographs and reams of descriptive writing. Fortunately, despite the rising mindless chauvinism of recent times, they have been allowed to survive, albeit with periodic insensitive additions which are often a blemish on their otherwise imposing appearance. They have also, on occasion, suffered the indignity of having their names changed. If only our history could be altered by these rather puerile attempts at donning acquired finery!

Like other Bombay residents who grew up under the shadow of these architectural gems, I too have grown to love them and, in some cases, not completely lost the original sense of awe that they produced in me as a child when I first became conscious of them. Some 15 or 20 years back, however, I discovered another facet of public architecture or artifacts that dot the city. Though infinitely less glamorous, they carry a great appeal for me. These are what might almost be called items of street furniture that once served a mundane, though necessary, purpose. Often they also recorded some little moment in the broad sweep of history that saw the growth of a large, teeming metropolis from a small settlement.

In the first category, in my list, are the old milestones on arterial roads leading north from south Bombay. These mark the distance in miles from St. Thomas' Church, as St. Thomas' Cathedral was earlier called. St. Thomas' is located adjacent to the old Elphinstone Circle, now called Horniman Circle. The Elphinstone Circle, the successor to the original Bombay Green was, in the 18th century, the centre of a growing city.

The city in those days was much smaller than it is today. These roads, so congested now, had their origins in the rides or paths which later became the roads leading out of Bombay. They must have run through what was originally virgin country, the milestones being the only locating markers. They may also have served as markers on roads linking different settlements, which in those days were separate but later absorbed into the growing city. Examples could be Sion, Sewri, Bandra and the far reaches of Nepean Sea Road.

These stones, originally at least three or four feet tall, are made from rough hewn basalt. Today they are buried much deeper with less than two feet protruding from the road or pavement surface. Most of them date back to the end of the 18th or the early 19th century. One is clearly more recent, as its inscription records the distance from St. Thomas' Cathedral. This indicates that it dates from a little before the middle of the 19th century, possibly later, i.e., after the church was elevated to the status of a cathedral. Today, you could pass it unnoticed, as it has been enveloped in old gunny bags put over it by the vegetable hawker who sits alongside.

Many years back, the Director of the Prince of Wales Museum (now the Chhatrapati Shivaji Maharaj Vastu Sangrahalaya) and I discussed whether all the milestones should be removed from their various locations and brought together into the grounds of the museum. (This has been done for the markers which showed the city limits of Bombay; they have been relocated outside the Bhau Daji Lad Museum, earlier called the Victoria and Albert Museum). His contention was that by doing so we could ensure their protection and hence preservation. I disagreed.

While endorsing his sentiment I felt that a milestone which had little aesthetic appeal, had real value only as a historic marker on a road that had come up over an old route. I also felt that a responsible and responsive city should try and preserve them in situ and arrange a modicum of protection for them where they stood. While this perhaps does not appear very practical, a large block of stone does not need much protection – only a little attention and concern. As events have turned out I wish I had accepted his advice. Sadly, I succeeded in convincing him and so he did not press his idea for relocating them with the authorities. One or two have since disappeared, while others have been damaged.

In some of the older parts of Bombay, often doing service as either bollards or protective posts, are old muzzle-loading cannon which are buried muzzle down with the breech end protruding above the pavement. After 1860, or thereabouts, developments in artillery made muzzle-loading cannon obsolete. Rifled barrelled, breach-loading cannon, firing streamlined projectiles, supplanted the older smooth bore cannon which fired spherical cannon balls or chain shot. Cast iron cannon became worthless and, therefore, since even the labour cost of moving them was not justified, they were either buried or 'used' where they were located. Cannon made from phosphor-bronze were obviously cut up or melted down for recycling the valuable alloy.

One comes across these cannon along some Bombay roads, sometimes in odd places. These are generally found in areas where there were troop lines or adjacent to where the old fort walls ran. One can be found not far from the location of the old Government House in the Parel area.

Excavations for building foundations or for provision of services below roads, coupled with road repair, occasionally unearth these cannon. A few years back two cannon were found when road work was carried out in front of the Metro cinema. These, along with cannon lying in the Azad Maidan, have been moved to the grounds of the Chhatrapati Shivaji Maharaj Vastu Sangrahalaya, the main Bombay museum. Many years ago when the foundation of the Reserve Bank of India's new tower block, adjacent to the mint, was being laid, a pair of very large guns were found. Since nobody wanted them and they were heavy, and therefore difficult to relocate, they were left where they were and the building constructed over them.

Some official buildings, with no martial connections, have taken these disused cannon and mounted them either on front lawns or at the gates in what is presumably an attempt to impress the populace with an imposing display of authority backed by force! The fact that the cannon have often been painted in a totally unsuitable colour has obviously escaped the attention of the powers that be!

Benefactors of the city often donated drinking water fountains which were either stand-alone or were combined with drinking water troughs for horses or cattle, reflective of an age where the only source of motive power was the use of draught animals. All over the city there are drinking fountains donated by people like Cowasjee Jehangir and Jamsetjee Jeejeebhoy. These come in many different shapes and sizes and have been made from a range of materials – granite, cast iron and masonry. Some of those donated by Cowasjee Jehangir were made in Scotland by A. MacDonald of Aberdeen in 1865 and sent out to India. Several must have been fabricated or cast locally in the foundries that came-up in the second half of the 19th century. Cowasjee gifted the city over 40 drinking fountains; I have only been able to find about half a dozen; it is fair to assume that many do not exist any longer.

In the early 1860s, when Sir Henry Bartle Frere was governor, the fort walls were razed to accommodate the rapidly burgeoning city and facilitate introduction of piped water supply. This ensured that reasonably potable water replaced water from tanks and wells which was often contaminated or disease spreading.

Commemorative fountains were also donated. The owners of private markets and stall holders of municipal markets in the Crawford Market, now the Mahatma Phule Market, donated a drinking fountain to commemorate the visit of their Imperial Majesties, King George V and Queen Mary in 1911, to Bombay. The market also has a magnificent fountain depicting the rivers of India designed by Lockwood Kipling, who was the dean of the Art School. He was the father of the celebrated author and poet of the *Raj*, Rudyard Kipling, incidentally born in the precincts of the Art School. Has our strong nationalism, tinged with a little chauvinism, made Rudyard Kipling – who has written affectionately, though with some condescension, about a now vanished period in our history – somewhat unpopular?

Fountains were also erected in memory of people such as the late Ramji Setiba funded by a donation received from the advocate general and in 1894 of Dharamsee Muljee, the only son of Ruttonsee Muljee. In 1894 a fountain was presented to the municipality of Bandra by Jafferbhai Ludha Khatu. There are other fountains, one in memory of a Dr. Parulkar in 1940 by his wife. Still another was presented to the municipality in memory of Seth Ramji Keshawji Contractor by his brother in 1943.

Several of these fountains have over the years been woefully neglected and are in a sorry state. Others have been vandalized either by miscreants or by the authorities. They evidently gave permission for a fountain – initially presented to the municipality in 1913, in memory of Seth Luxmidas Kothari and his wife Nanibai by their son Madhavdas Luxmidas Kothari – to be converted and partially remade in memory of Shri and Smt. Fakirchand Vohra of Khushab, Sargoda (W. Pakistan) under the auspices of the Bombay Citizen Committee. This is now enveloped in junk that the municipality has dumped around it.

At one time, in perhaps a more refined age, it would appear that to commemorate a memory one donated a facility to the city. Today, in a more materialistic age, it seems easier to enter into a private 'treaty' with the municipality and either change the old, and therefore traditional and historic, name of a street or get any intersection of streets designated a *chowk* and name it after someone.

One great source of pleasure for me has been locating old plaques which mark significant events in the development of the city or commemorate noteworthy occurrences. One plaque in Colaba marks the spot from where, prior to 1838, the ferry went for a distance of 300 yards from the island of Bombay to Old Woman's Island. As part of the scheme to link the seven islands of Bombay, this creek was filled up; that was the end of the ferry service. The road built, Colaba Causeway, is now called Shaheed Bhagat Singh Road. Another plaque in the Mahim area records the making of the Mahim Causeway linking the main island to Bandra. It credits Lady Jeejeebhoy, the main donor.

There is an old building in a busy, bustling area near the stock exchange which once served, from 1757 until 1829, as the residence of the Governor of Bombay. Later, from 1829 to 1873, it became the Secretariat. A plaque, now mostly hidden by a mound of scrap paper, informs us that this was the home of Governor Jonathan Duncan who died here in 1811. A plaque in another building tells us that it was formerly known as Admiralty House as it was the residence of the Admiral from 1764 to 1792. In 1800 it became the Court of the First Recorder of Bombay and remained the Chief Court of Bombay until the establishment of the High Court in 1879.

Various public buildings carry plaques telling us about their foundation and building cost. It is amazing to read how well the costs were controlled, and usually managed within budget! In some cases a little history also appears on the plaque. The plaque on St. Thomas' Cathedral is particularly rewarding. In the 19th century, when many public buildings came up, the plaques carried a lot of information on dates, costs and the name of the architect and sometimes that of the principal contractor.

The plaques sometimes bear testimony to small changes or events in history. A plaque on Waudby Road (now Somani Marg) records the bravery of Major Sidney James Waudby, who with Private Elahi Bux and Private Somnak Tannak in April 1880 defended the Dubrai post in Afghanistan for three hours against 300 enemy. When their ammunition was exhausted they dashed into the midst of their foes and died fighting. The tablet was placed by their regiment, the 19th BP Infantry, to commemorate their heroism. This plaque was originally on the outer wall of a girls school building and was visible from the street. When the building was razed and then redeveloped, the plaque was moved to the side of the new building and is now not visible from the road, placed as it is behind a high compound wall!

Plaques on bridges, particularly those over the GIP Railway (now Central Railway,) show the development of the east-west links of the city, which is largely linear with a north-south alignment. One road was built by a 'multitude of people driven from Surat in 1793 in that year of famine.' The necessary funding was raised by public subscription. This was a famine relief measure to provide employment to mitigate hardship, and is perhaps an early example of impoverished peoples gravitating to Bombay in search of a livelihood, a trend which continues to date.

Outside the PWD office is the stone which records the Standard Benchmark for Bombay. It captures the history of recording tide levels between January 1878 and January 1885 at Apollo Bunder and goes on to record the highest tide height. Do present builders, or even the authorities, have regard for this or equivalent data when laying drainage lines or restoring sewers?

Bombay has, on its streets, a variety of fire hydrants of different vintage. These presumably date to the time when the city was growing and being modernized. A side benefit of a continuous water supply was that a hydrant system, essential for effective fire fighting, could now be introduced. Bombay has many different kinds of hydrants and I feel rewarded every time I come across one with a design different from others that I have seen before. One tall hydrant, approximately five feet high, has a fluted circumference and stands in the very heart of south Bombay. Generally it ends up being used as a post for displaying a hawker's wares. I have only come across one other like it and that is in a different part of town.

Artefacts, even as mundane as sewer vents, can be items of more than passing interest. The old ones are very tall and made from cast iron. These were put up when the city basically consisted of bungalows or two or three storey buildings, to vent obnoxious sewer gases away from the populace. They still stand, albeit a little rusted on the surface, not much the worse for wear. Their modern day replacements are half the height, that too in a predominately high-rise city! Aesthetically far less attractive, they are made out of poor quality concrete which is cracking and crumbling.

Old wrought iron railings are usually very appealing; sadly many of them have been damaged with pieces broken off them. They have been replaced by strip metal railings which are effective but infinitely uglier.

In recent years I have not come across anything new. No doubt there are objects still waiting to be 'discovered', but I cannot be sure. For some time now I have observed a large block of stone that is embedded in the pavement. It is fluted on two sides and has one face that is difficult to see as it is close to a railing which prevents one from examining it. This face, which is bounded by flutes, might have some worn-out wording on it. Could this be something special or merely a piece of coping from an old building? I cannot yet say, but I am working on it.

Matheran

RATAN K. LALKAKA

> *'Oh! Matheran Hill is fair to behold,*
> *Its water is pure and its breeze ice cold,*
> *The views from the Points well deserve admiration*
> *And the English delight in this lovely hill station.'*
>
> (A translation from a collection of songs gathered on the Hill.)

FOR the stressed out, the fatigued in mind and body, the tired and weary, there are few places like Matheran for a quick and effective rejuvenation of the senses and a mending of tattered nerves – enabling one to meet the world once again with a lighter and fresher step.

If one looks directly eastward from Bombay during early morning one will see a low hill silhouetted against the rising sun. It is Matheran.

Matheran rises sheer from the plains up to its highest point of 2600 ft, a mere 22 miles from Bombay as the crow flies, within easy reach of those who wish to delve into its beauty and charm and savour its clean and fresh air even for just a weekend. An early resident, Mrs. Oliver, in her definitive book on Matheran published in

1905 writes: 'Here lies the modest, yet fascinating little sanatorium of Matheran, whose claim to be one of the prettiest hill stations in India has long been undisputed. There are, indeed, many travellers who assert that the peculiar beauty of its sylvan glades and wide prospects over the surrounding country will compare with any scenery to be found in the world. The name Matheran is at once expressive and explanatory... on the top a forest.'

The hill station was discovered in 1850 by Hugh Poyntz Malet, then collector of Thana, who made the ascent from the village of Chowk to the top of the hill and was immediately impressed with its natural beauty. Having apparently fallen in love with his discovery, he soon returned to the hill and made several subsequent visits when he took up his friends and relatives who built simple dab and wattle huts. In 1855 the Governor of Bombay, Lord Elphinstone, visited the hill and for him it was love at first sight. With its salubrious climate and its proximity to Bombay he foresaw Matheran's popularity.

In the early days, before the cart road from Neral to Matheran was constructed and the railway connected Bombay to Neral, a person wishing to reach Matheran had a laborious journey ahead of him. He took a ferryboat from Bombay to Ulva, a small *bunder* across the harbour, from where he took a *tonga* to Panvel, a small town a few miles inland and then rode a bullock cart to Chowk, the same village from where Malet had jumped off to 'discover' Matheran. From Chowk, the traveller climbed up to Matheran via the same trail traversed by Malet.

Later, when the then GIP Railway on its way to Poona reached Neral in 1854, the journey became quicker and less laborious. Still later, in 1907, when Sir Adamji Peerbhoy built the Matheran Light Railway with a gauge of two feet and a total distance of 14 miles from Neral to the hill station, the journey from Bombay to Matheran became even quicker and more comfortable. It was now possible to reach Matheran within four hours from Victoria Terminus.

The commissioning of the Ghat Road from Neral to Matheran and government commencing the allotment of plots for residential purposes had a salutary effect on the progress of the hill. Plots were leased out at Rs 5 per acre per annum with a limit of five acres for each lessee. The stipulation was that the plot boundary walls be kept low to facilitate the passage of animals. The progress of the hill station was now rapid, the 17 bungalows of 1867 rising to more than 200 in 1950, the majority of them built in colonial style with wide verandas sweeping around. A little township with a bazaar emerged along Matheran's main road consisting of residential places, hotels and lodging houses, shops, bakeries and restaurants. A dispensary and a hospital came up, space for horse stables was allocated, all this to serve the tourist and the residents of the far-flung bungalows. The villagers came up the hill to sell local produce in the Sunday bazaar, making a colourful contribution to the proceedings.

Gymkhanas were established for games and provided entertainment and amusement for the steadily growing number of visitors. A Protestant church, St. Pauls, was consecrated in 1865, almost at the same time as the Roman Catholic one, to cater to the spiritual needs of the visitors. A mosque was erected in 1872. Several Hindu temples were also built; though the Pisharnath temple near the lake was in existence much before Malet even came up.

An enterprising family, Ms. Jai F. Mehta and sisters, published a little magazine on the Hill, *Matheran Jottings*, twice each week during the season between mid-April and the beginning of June. It was a unique publication, giving news of the Hill covering events that had occurred and were forthcoming. It encapsulated all that happened during that brief period.

Regrettably, I have been able to lay my hands on only one issue – that of May 1916. One learns from the columns of Matheran Jottings that Sir Pherozshah Mehta loved Matheran and spent many hours of his long life on the hill. Matheran's popularity grew and it soon became Bombay's favourite hill station where people sought refuge away from the hustle and bustle and from its stifling heat. If Malet was the founder of Matheran then Lord Elphinstone was the founder of its prosperity and popularity.

On reaching the top, by road or rail, one is soon in a thick forest which, with its ambience of total peace, is not unlike that of paradise. The first impact as you enter is as if a door to an airconditioned room has been opened and you are enveloped in a delicious coolness. In exhilaration you walk on. Matheran's top is a small plateau of about 3.8 sq. miles, undulating and irregular, being a narrow uneven tableland with rocky headlands known as Points. The annual rainfall of 250-300 inches maintains this evergreen forest of trees and shrubs which is sustained by a thick layer of porous red laterite stone which acts like a huge sponge from which the roots of the evergreens drink deep throughout the year.

The forest lies like a mantle over the hill through which the founders laid out walks that are shady even during the summer midday sun and which encourage you to walk on. The walks hug the contours and usually end at the rocky headlands commanding magnificent views of the surrounding valleys and hills. Openings in the forest called 'Griffiths Peeps' were made and designed for obtaining marvellous views from various angles. The scenery of the unfolding valleys is breathtaking and never fails to awe anyone who takes in the scene. The sunsets are always wonderful to witness, particularly during October when the atmosphere is washed and clean and the masses of clouds on the western horizon turn to orange and red as the sun descends to meet the sea.

Walks are the pleasantest and most rewarding pursuit on the hill. Francesa Wilson in 'My Trip to Matheran' said of this hill station:

'It is like an enormous wood or jungle, with seventy miles of roads cut through it. The stranger who starts out for a walk, imagines he is alone with the mountain solitude, with no dwelling near him. He is charmed with the varied foliage, and splendid trees gnarled with age, that he frequently passes. Each turn in the winding road discovers more and more beauties, avenues of lofty trees forming arched roofs... His astonishment when he visits these Points is extreme; he walks along guided by the numerous sign-posts, little thinking what is in store for him. He sees no opening in the wood until close on to the

Point, when suddenly he finds himself with the grandest scenery in front of him.'

On a walk, besides coming across a galloping horse or troops of monkeys on their aerial paths up above in the trees or down on the forest floor foraging for food, there is nothing else to disturb one's peace of mind. The early British had wisely banned the automobile from ever coming upon the hill (a ban which is still in existence, making Matheran Asia's only car-free hill station) and no internal combustion engine pollutes the pristine atmosphere. The fresh air is invigorating and after just a couple of days one's steps become springier and there is a decided difference in the level of fitness. Nature is absorbed into one's physical being, producing a totally relaxed feeling.

Another pleasant occurrence is the morning birdsong; just after dawn, in the jungle all around you, the birds seem to wake up in unison with a song to herald the waking day. Sweet melodies and lilting tunes colour the morning air – the thrush, the robin, the bulbul, the whistling schoolboy in season and many others sing to their hearts content just for a short while before breaking into silence once again.

During Matheran's earlier and halcyon days, the style and desires of holiday makers were quite different from todays vacationers whose visits are primarily of a much shorter duration. Such was the pull of Matheran for us as children that we wasted no time in reaching it once school closed for the summer vacation. We took a train from Victoria Terminus to Neral and then climbed up to the Hill and home to 'Woodlands', a bungalow at Porcupine Point, a total walk of about three and half to four hours. Our happy vacation regrettably came to an end once the monsoon arrived during the beginning of June – exactly on time. In those days even nature kept to her schedule!

Our entire holiday was spent walking, riding, reading, listening to music and exploring the nearby hills. We enjoyed each and every day spent in the pursuit of nature and marvelling at her creations. The several gymkhanas were alive with games and tournaments and a fair degree of socializing enlivened the season as each bungalow entertained in style. This kind of life reached its peak just after the Second World War when the more affluent could not go abroad and had to congregate in Matheran for their holidays.

Although Matheran's altitude is not high when compared to other hill stations, it is relatively cooler because of the thick forests and its closeness to the sea. April is hot but by mid-May coolness pervades the atmosphere and a few showers further lower the temperature. By the end of May clouds begin gathering, announcing the monsoon which arrives bang on cue. The period from end-May till the arrival of the monsoon is perhaps the most beautiful and spectacular on the hill. Mists rise up from the valley and shroud the hill; occasional showers and thunderstorms arrive in the evenings and then the monsoon hits Matheran, not in a gradual or gentle manner but in a series of gigantic thunderclaps and lightning.

From being hot and muggy, a delicious moist coolness envelopes the hill and the smell of fresh earth fills the nostrils. The coming of the monsoon, though a rebirth for the hill, signals the end of the season for the visitor and the tourist. The monsoon is very hard for the few inhabitants who perforce have to continue residence; everything remains damp, clothes do not dry and often it rains without pause for days on end. The continued cutting of trees has however decreased the rainfall from an average of more than 300 inches per year in the early 1900s to less than 200 inches now.

Let us now take a walk through the leafy paths of the hill station visiting several of its many Points and places of general interest which existed just after the war. Unaided by illustrations or photographs and in this case even by a map, words are inadequate to describe the hill's sheer beauty and loveliness.

For no particular reason, but taking it as a central point of the hill, let us start at the Matheran Railway Station. Once a focus of great social activity as one rushed to meet the trains coming from Neral to check out who had arrived, there is now no such excitement and the arrival of a train has become a routine affair.

We walk on Matheran's 'main road' alongside the railway track northwards till we turn east, leaving the road and the railway to go down to Neral. We pass Beatrice Cliff, a wooded bluff with a pretty view of a valley and proceed onto the easterly point of Garbut. This point appears to be at the end of a separate hill and the view gives a vista of the many ranges and villages that lie to the east, including Lonavla with its 'Dukes Nose' rearing up.

From Garbut we walk to Panorama Point, Matheran's northern most point affording a sweeping vista of the east, west and the north. The view is indeed magnificent and worth the walk.

We double back and walk southwards but now on Matheran's westerly flank, we pass Hart Point and Monkey Point, both with lovely views. We pass Elphinstone Lodge, an estate of more than 30 acres, the largest on the Hill. It was built in 1858 or thereabouts by Lord Elphinstone and still retains its original charm. Westwards now we go, passing the European Gymkhana which once boasted of six tennis courts and Malet Spring, so named after the hill's Founder. Before the advent of Charlotte Lake and a piped water supply to the bungalows, water was collected from the various springs and carried by *bhistis* in *pakhals* made of buffalo skin.

From Malet Spring on to Porcupine Point, in my view the prettiest point on the hill. It has an unbroken view of a circle of hills from Panorama Point to Bawa Malang, all in an arc. The valley below is aptly named Maldoonga, literally a necklace of hills. On a clear day, especially after the monsoon when the atmosphere is clean and washed, the island of Bombay lies shimmering with its high buildings clearly visible. Unfortunately, with today's pollution this is not possible. The sunsets are a joy to behold.

From Porcupine now walk southwards to Louisa Point from where again the view towards the west is magnificent. A promontory bearing a marked resemblance to a lion's head is named so and is typical of these odd rock formations found elsewhere in the western ghats. Matheran's sister hill Prabal runs alongside, a smaller hill in area but of the same height. Sir George Birdwood in his autobiography

Sva mentions the sunsets seen from Louisa as the most poetic thing he encountered in life.

From Louisa you turn eastwards and then south towards Lake Charlotte, once Matheran's main source of water. Today, water is pumped up from the Ulhas river but before that happened the length of your holiday in summer often depended on how long the water in the lake lasted! Across the lake lies Pisarnath temple, the foremost sanctuary in Matheran. People believe that Pisarnath can bestow favours like those attributed to shrines elsewhere.

As Matheran became the venue of fashionable society the need for a racecourse was felt. Olympia, as it is called, lies on a flat piece of land as we walk southwards. The Bombay Amateur Riders Club hold their annual mounted sports at Olympia over the last two weekends of May.

You now walk to One Tree Hill so named for the obvious reason that it has always only had one tree growing on it. Go to the two southernmost points, Little Chowk and Big Chowk, and make an about turn and return to the bazaar. That completes a circle of Matheran. A good walker can 'do' the whole Hill in less than a couple of days.

Regrettably, starting from about the 1960s a great change started sweeping over the once lovely hill. Because of its proximity to Bombay and Poona, with growing affluence more and more people started visiting the Hill. Matheran came under the avaricious gaze of 'developers' anxious to cash in on this tourist boom. Official statistics place the average daily influx of the floating population at 10,000 in 1996 compared to 4000 in 1977. Matheran's ecologically sensitive region came under tremendous pressure from overbuilding of lodges and hotels.

To accommodate this rush, hotels proliferated and were built without regulations or rules. The worst that could have happened to the Hill happened – an onslaught on the environment. Trees were felled illegally and indiscriminately and the forest cover began thinning, resulting in an increase in temperatures.

Today, the Hill faces water shortages, periodic failure of electricity, traffic congestion and other pressures on its fragile infrastructure. There was also a determined attempt by vested interests to lift the ban on motor cars entering the township. Luckily for Matheran and its lovers, these attempts were thwarted and the ban stays.

Efforts made by local environmental groups have resulted in the government issuing a notification which declared Matheran and its surrounds an eco-sensitive zone. Lovers of nature and particularly of Matheran now pray and hope that the provisions of this notification will become effective and enable Matheran to be restored to its original beauty and glory. I end with another translation from a collection of songs gathered on the Hill:

> 'The delightful shade of this garden is fitted to remove fatigue,
> the cuckoos, parrots and other birds singing melodiously,
> how much do they tranquillise this troubled mind!
> The spray issuing from the playing fountain joins
> the wind laden with the scent of flowers.'

A community at the crossroads

PHEROZA GODREJ

'Oh dear Mumbai, my dear Mumbai.
Tu Fort Market hathi
Have tu black market thai gai.
Vakhat avo hatho, ke bagal ma bairi lai,
Vakhat avo aiyo, ke bairi pun gul thai gai.'

(Oh dear Mumbai – my dear Mumbai, once upon a time you were identified by the Fort Market. Unfortunately, now you are well known as a city of the black market, it has become your identity in the world today. There was a time when it was safe to walk around the streets holding the wife's hand, but today, the situation is such that you could loose your wife while walking down the streets.)

THUS, Fali Master, a popular dramatist who performed to packed audiences in the Lalbaug, Parel, and Byculla localities of Bombay in the 1950s, expressed the despair and the insecurity felt by the middle class Parsis of Bombay. India had just 'stepped out of the old into the new' as Nehru so eloquently put it and the task of national reconstruction had not yet fully begun. It is not possible to elaborate why Fali Master's Parsis were a worried lot, but a closer look at the

* I would like to gratefully acknowledge the many hours of conversation with Rusheed R. Wadia, a city-based economic historian and Cyrus Phiroze Shroff, a city-based software engineer.

broader social history of Bombay may yield a few answers. What is noteworthy is that a tone of uncertainty slowly crept into the earlier expression of Parsi power and glory.

A certain uniformness appeared in the great melting pot of globalization and, in Mumbai, one could not at a glance distinguish persons of any particular community. However, if we went back in time, say even 10 years, the word 'bawa' or 'bawi' conjured up an image of a man, the quintessential Parsi male, attired in a white trouser wearing a white long coat known as the 'dagla', under which he wore, close to his skin, the sacred vest – the 'sadra' – over which he tied around his waist the 'kasti', followed by a buttoned-up white shirt and a traditional head gear – he had a choice of three – the *padgi*, the *pheta* or a simple velvet *topi* resembling a skull cap.

Bombay is a city which has transformed or more appropriately reinvented itself in the last half century. Among the various communities that have made Bombay their home, the Parsis were at the forefront. From almost two centuries ago when they were invited by the British to come and ply their trade in this fledgling seaport, they have been leaders in many activities and professions.

The key to Parsi survival, wherever this community has laid down their roots has been adaptability. Tolerance of others is an intrinsic part of their identity. While religion and cultural elements should be part of the Parsi identity, it must be Indianess at the centre. The buildings that one sees as one drives through Bombay – Elphinstone College, Capital Cinema, J.J. School of Art and Architecture, J.J. Hospital, The Bai Sakarbai Dinshaw Petit Hospital for Animals, the Institute for Science, the Cowasji Jehangir Hall, as well as the Mahim Causeway – were among the many established by Parsis for the cosmopolitan needs of the city.

Today, with an increase of educated in all communities and the strong spirit of competitiveness in the work force placed by world demands, the Parsi youth, by and large, have not shown the entrepreneurial skills of their forefathers. What does the statement 'I am a Parsi' mean in the commercial world? Of course it immediately represents trust and you will find many a Parsi working as a teller in a bank or as an auditor in a multi-national accounts firm – these are traditional proofs.

More than 50 years later, uncertainties of a different sort prevail. But, the distorted representation of Parsis, time and again, as buffoons, wimps and cranks in films and advertizing commercials raises disturbing questions. Does this image reflect an underlying larger crisis confronting the community? In what follows, I shall reflect on some of these issues.

The Parsis, whose journey out of the villages of Gujarat began over 150 years ago had by the late 19th century firmly set their imprint on the making of Bombay. They had, of course, been around much longer as itinerant traders from the early 18th century. In the mid 19th century they played a big role not only in India's effort at industrialization, but most importantly in the setting up of infrastructure in Bombay.

By the early 20th century, the Parsis of Bombay were residing in community financed housing. The mill owning family of Wadia promoted the Baugs (Parsi colonies) in a big way. These acts of philanthropy are visible all over the island city stretching from Cusrow Baug in Colaba, Jer Baug, Rustom Baug and Ness Baug in Central Bombay, right up to Malcom Baug in Jogeshwari.

The first two Baugs developed in the 1920s are singular examples of apartment buildings in the art deco style. The last one comprises spacious bungalows, some two stories high. The grounds are laid out not only with large avenues lined with shade giving trees and adequate car parking (a space whose value has skyrocketed in Bombay), gardens for recreation, volleyball and football facilities, pavilions for indoor sports and social events, some Baugs even have Fire Temples within their precincts.

Although this community housing is a boon, it tends to generate a 'ghetto' mentality. In contrast to the low housing provided by other communities in what is referred to as 'chawls', the Parsis lived very differently and this led to a certain feeling of distinctiveness. The 'bawa baugs' and the 'ghati chawls' (those who resided in the western ghats) or the 'miya mohallahs' were all the same. Yet, five decades ago, immediately after independence, the tension of partition resounded in these pockets of community dwellings. In 1992-93, when the fabric of Bombay's physical and emotional life was devastated by communal riots, the Parsis living in the baugs were almost paralyzed. Their gates, which normally had their ornate wrought iron grills open 24 hours a day, suddenly acquired the image of fortresses with 24 hour security being maintained.

By the late 19th century, Parsis and other communities in Bombay had specific localities marked out for them as residential sites. The process of dismantling earlier more cosmopolitan space in the city had been going on for quite some time. These developments of the second half of the 19th century were to have far reaching consequences in the social life of the different communities of Bombay.

While the advantages of community subsidized housing are self-evident, the insularity this can promote has not been focused upon. Rohinton Mistry provides a window to this problem in his celebrated *Tales from Ferozeshah Baug*. He shows how living within community enclaves with a restricted interaction with other communities in the neighbourhood is potentially alienating. Such alienation can get exacerbated at times of communal tensions and especially during riots. That greater efforts must be made to enhance integration between communities needs open discussion and is a well-established sociological recommendation. As far as I can perceive there is absolutely no reason why Parsis must keep away from this vital social necessity.

Health care has played an important role. Indeed the roster and reputation of Parsi doctors is legendary. Again, charity plays an important role and the geriatric ward at the Parsi General Hospital is never empty. With the middle class, the backbone of any community, in which all members of the family work, there is no one to take care of the old and sick. This hospital is a boon to the aged of this community.

In the years gone by, the Parsi medical fraternity would have an annual play in which they whole heartedly participated, acting, to raise funds for the free wards at the hospital. The plays were hilarious, poking fun at ourselves. This is a healthy trend for any community as it keeps one aware of ones many foibles. In the hospital, the death rate is higher than the birth rate, causing grave concern in the community. Arithmetic says we will die out if we don't first address, second debate, and third preserve our community without losing our identity. This is one of the more serious problems facing our community, not only in Bombay but all over the world.

Apart from community financed housing and health care, education was another important component of the social project of the Parsi community. Looking back nearly two centuries, development of education, at the outset only for males, was central to the community building project. In the mid 19th century, efforts to educate women also began. Dosebai Jessawalla's classic *The Story of My Life* documents in detail the struggle for womens' education in this period. Education across this whole century was accompanied by a vigorous movement for social reform not just within the Parsi community, but in the larger Indian context also.

One can hardly forget Nowroji Chandaru's *Chabook* (Whip) which had a reputation for not pulling its punches when it came to exposing corruption in the Parsi Punchayet in 1830. Equally distinguished was the mid 19th century publication, the *Rast Goftar*, a vehicle of enlightened opinion and which, while contesting conservative opinion, regularly bared the sores of Parsi society. In this task it had the satirical writings of the *Parsee Punch* (1854) as an ally. In 1958, the Parsee Punch widened its influence when it became the *Hindi Punch*.

No less influential in its critical impact was Parsi theatre. The English and vernacular Gujarati theatre patronized took a close by the Parsis look at the seamy underside of Parsi and Indian society. The Magicians performed by the Parsi Theatrical Company (founded in 1853) remains an important cultural event for examining the guile and deceit of Brahmins towards Indian women.

A 150 years later, the cultural world of the Parsi is hardly as illuminating and vigorous as it was in the late 19th and early 20th century. Economic backwardness continues to plague the small minority: the condition of widows, aged and infirm among them being especially deplorable.

A significant number of Parsis continue to patronize occult and pseudo-religious practices. The enormous popularity of the Gururani Naagmata cult, with a following among Parsis and non-Parsis, situated in a prominent Parsi colony of Bombay, has even led to a road being named after it. Similarly, Parsis flock to Mount Mary, a Roman Catholic domain; the Darga at Haji Ali, a Muslim stronghold; the Sai Baba complex at Shridi, a Hindu pilgrimage site. I question, why? What is it that is lacking in our own faith that we need to look elsewhere? I truly believe that for the majority it is a lack of knowledge of our own faith. Who is to be blamed for this? Even if the clergy has not helped in bringing the community closer into the fold, surely as individuals we could educate ourselves a little bit more on the legacy that we have been born into.

But it is the endless tension within the community over the issues of intermarriage and disposal of the dead which is urgently crying out for attention. We need to openly discuss changes in our attitudes towards marriage outside the fold. It raises the complex issue of genetics. What we need to preserve for the development of the community is our cultural identity so admired by the world. That is what is important. The supremacy of reason and humanism promotes a culture of continual inquiry about the physical and social world we inhabit.

The physical world we must use with care; equally preserve the social world. We must seek to understand and organize rationally so as to build societies that are free of want and which will promote the intellectual and cultural development of its members.

Hitherto, a great deal of rancour has accompanied the interminable discussions and altercations discussed in the Parsi press, official bodies and public meetings. No consensus on any issue has emerged so far. That this should happen in a community as small as the Parsis, is surprising and painful.

The community is so divided that it is never able to discuss other equally pertinent issues. At this stage one must point out to people unfamiliar with the community that even though the core which binds them is the religion, there is a cultural difference between Zoroastrians of Iran and the Zoroastrians of India. In India, this small community has fully integrated itself into the national fabric. You will find a Parsi in practically every walk of life. In Iran, during the regime of the late Mohammed Reza Shah Pahlavi, the above mentioned statement was also true.

Today, although Iranian Zoroastrians live in peace, they are segregated by the fact that they live in a predominantly agrarian society. They continue to till land and are engaged in simple trades such as carpentry and weaving as practiced by their forefathers. It is therefore important that Parsis within India and without should amicably resolve these matters through debate and discussion.

When striving to do so, if one looks for suggestions from history, an important lesson emerges. The careers of all those distinguished 19th century Parsis like Dadabhai Naoroji, Sorabji Bengallee, Dinshaw Wacha, and others teaches us that those who succeeded in offering creative solutions to the community's problems were also striving for solutions to the problems of the larger Indian nation. The enormous importance of such a wider perspective should not be lost sight of by those who wish to take the Parsi community ahead.

For the last 100 years and specifically after independence, the Zoroastrian community in India has wrestled with many issues threatening its existence. In this fast changing world, where does this minuscule people numbering a hundred-thousand stand? In times gone by the strength of the community lay focused in parts of western India and north eastern Iran. Today, several factors are promoting their migration from these strongholds.

The diaspora is virtually on every continent, with well established communities in North America, the United Kingdom, Hong Kong and the fledgling but growing one between Australia and New Zealand. Other than coming together from time to time to celebrate events such as Federation meetings and World Congresses, the community rarely meets. However, thanks to the internet, communication has increased. This is a wonderful tool and ought to be used in a positive fashion.

Contemplating the future of the community, I feel we have got into a rut. No people can hope to grow unless there is a vision. We seem to have got embroiled in issues which should have been settled long back.

The Parsis are at a critical juncture. After having survived 3500 years, we must look forward to flourishing in the next millennium with righteousness and hard work by following the simple three tenets of the Zoroastrian faith: 'Good Thoughts, Good Words, and Good Deeds.' These values, like the perpetual fire, must be kept burning in our hearts and minds.

An expat's eye

ANABEL LOYD

HISTORICALLY the expatriates arriving in Bombay dreamt, if not of streets paved with gold, at least of rich rewards. Like the street kids who nowadays throng Victoria Terminus, they came to scavenge and compete to realize a dream and all too often found themselves competing against impossible obstacles, suffering and dying in the attempt. The contemporary arrival still has to fight to find a niche in a clogged city of 15 million souls in which even the soft cushion of corporate status and padded expense account is not absolute proof against the red tape, raw character and dysfunction of this welling mass of life.

Entering this cacophonous environment engenders similar sensations to the confusion of mind wrought by the first pages of a great Russian novel. A whirl of characters, names, threads of relationships familial and financial, great business houses or their relics, historical importances glorified in barely noticed statues and memorials. A multicultured conglomeration of individuals living at a crossroads of history, trade and money. A magnet for the actual or potential entrepreneur ready to snatch his moment of opportunity or luck. Bombay, like other cities built on finance and the promise of wealth is home to the individual. Lines of dependence exist but they are always stretching and mutating as each character creates his or her own path through the labyrinth. Less than any other city in India where apparently the key is community, here the individual rules and has the self-belief to build his own kingdom in a competitive empire.

In the past the expatriate who triumphed over climate, disease and misadventure succeeded often far beyond his expectations. Riches and power were the prizes. As in other erstwhile jewels in colonial crowns the myth endures and has, until recent years, continued to find solid substance, not perhaps in the swelling coffers of the nabob but those of the international corporation. Now, although the outside adventurers and invaders have left their many marks on the structure and spirit of Bombay, they have little part to play in the life of the city. Outside influence has been and continues to be disseminated and absorbed but modernization of all kinds is coming from within at least as much as without. This energy of ideas combined with a traditional work ethic has created a reverse colonization by NRIs, as successful financially and intellectually, if not yet politically as that of Victorian empirebuilders.

A day in Bombay offers to the traveller a sample cutting of the fabric of the contemporary city. For one who visited first only in the late eighties or early nineties, the cloth of the city may seem unchanging but the moving spirit is thrusting towards the future, however veiled it may be. Sahara airport, the heaving slum of Dharavi and gluelike traffic notwithstanding, the first major sight in Bombay for the transient remains the Gateway of India with its attendant hustling throng and then the splendid bulk of the Taj Mahal Hotel. Constant upgrading and modernizing has kept the Taj among the great hotels of the world and, despite of the dubious architectural appeal of the new building, it is still a more imposing landmark than most.

The Taj and Oberoi hotels remain major meeting places for business people and well-heeled travellers but recently increasing numbers of international style bars and restaurants have grabbed their slice of the action. Where once there were a handful of designer restaurants in South Bombay, now there are new 'in' places round every corner and far into the suburbs too. An international flavour has taken over where Trishna and Khyber ruled supreme and Chinese, European and South-East Asian cooking awaits only the whim of current fashion.

'Designer' rules, at least for the gilded young of the city and, at this level, Bombay becomes like every other international stopping point. Jewellers touting for the tourist trade no longer settle for the traditional tribal bangles and beads beloved by travellers of the sixties and seventies. The latest designs could be found anywhere in Europe or America. Bombay has a plethora of exciting designers who may have digested details from other cultures but now have more innovative ideas to export than they desire or need to import.

As a glance in the window of an elegant boutique in London or New York will demonstrate, Indian influence and designer style is now conquering the highest end of the market as much as the sixties that once cornered the cheap trade. The expatriate can come and buy with his welcome dollars (India is enduringly fashionable and still cheap) but he has little to offer in terms of ideas that is more creative, exciting or just new. Bombay looked like a dusty dowager, now she is kicking off the crinoline and elbowing her way to the front line of fashion. The evidence is easy to find, even on that first journey from the airport, in the flashy splashy glossy magazines sold by street boys at your car window.

The street children begging or selling in and out of the traffic, the pathetic beggars and their apathetic babies ever tapping on the glass for alms are no less a part of the Bombay dream than the designer babes in cool Colaba bars. The 'individual' city is a hard place, increasingly upbeat and forward looking but still dysfunctional and difficult and not too many safety nets available for anyone. Street kids come following their dream; beggars are a symbol of the sea of poverty surrounding this island of wealth in a developing country. Seagulls follow fishing boats, beggars follow money, nothing changes.

The street child is something different; he or she has a vision and because he is a child with the hopes of children, he expects ultimately to get his chance for success. The brutality of Bombay, the battle for survival, creates a craving for any comfort or release from the struggle. For street kids the comfort comes mostly from ultimately destructive pleasures; drugs provide the cheapest and most available form of escape. Work with children in these circumstances is hardly a fashion role but certainly one with as much scope for new ideas as in any shiny design studio.

North America and Europe have long felt themselves to be the leaders in charity to the developing world and, whilst better financial controls and organization are devoutly to be desired at both ends of the donor line, this is still a vital if disappointing state of affairs. However, in new concepts or the ability to think laterally and work out creative and fitting methodologies, small organizations all over India and noticeably in Bombay are far ahead. Unfortunately the constant cult of the individual, the ubiquitous handicap of small non-governmental organizations, slows the procreation and nurturing of these ideas through competitive bickering and one upmanship between interested parties.

A more opaque form of social competition seems to be a mark of cities built on trade and finance with an indigenous and expatriate meritocracy, quite outside the traditional order of caste and class, of those who have scrambled to the top of the pyramid. In all such societies and perhaps particularly those whose geography makes them to some extent self-contained islands, there is constant competition to prove financial and social standing. Bombay today has the same indicators of success at every level of society as similar cities round the globe. Ranging from the just acquired trendy trainers, the cable television set or two, up through the motorcycle, motor car, the Mercedes, a room, a house, a penthouse apartment, then designer food and clothes, foreign travel, villas, the best of everything.

People have always enjoyed flaunting their achievements, aspiring to the possessions of those on higher rungs of the ladder and creating envy in those on the lower. At certain moments governments have passed sumptuary laws to quell such extravagant demonstration and encourage the use of resources for the common good. It is perhaps regrettable that when style and fashion overlay the substance of community tradition and culture, to possess the latest cell phone may be the overwhelming ambition of the A grade student.

Artistic prowess emerges where there are patrons and publicity. In the constant search for the new and exotic, contemporary Indian artists have taken an important place in the famous auction houses of the world. Buyers in Europe know for instance of the notoriety of Hussain and appreciate the dreamy beauty of a work of Anjoli Ela Menon and galleries have sprung up in Bombay in the wake of shows and sales in the great hotels. Bombay has always absorbed and embraced artistic movements and ideas; Victorian gothic, the bizarre mix of the Indo-Saracenic, the perfect examples of newly renovated art deco blocks. Now in fine art and architecture the ideas are coming from within the city and India and encouraged by internal patronage are adding to the top end of the quality export list.

It is likewise impossible to be unaware of the sparkling gewgaws of Bollywood on show to a worldwide audience. Dance extravaganzas on satellite television, 'Bombay Dreams' on stage, fusion music on pop radio stations, all reaching far beyond the NRI community. Bollywood directors and stars are becoming well-known faces and names in foreign magazines and newspapers and metamorphosing into international celebrities on the pages of *Hello* and *OK*.

That the world is a small place is the greatest cliché. India has for centuries been pushed and pussed by outside forces, empires have come and gone and left their marks. In the past few decades greater wealth has massively increased the numbers of the young middle classes able to travel, study and work outside India and leave their own marks on their adopted countries in return. The ticket to a US or occasionally still UK university is the golden dream of Bombay youth and the opportunity once received is well used. Most of the great scientific and medical research centres in the developed world use and value the brain-power, ambition and work ethic of these students.

The Indian education system may be hidebound and old fashioned with rote learning at the core but it manages to produce the inventive and advanced thinkers needed by global science and industry. Education in Bombay is as competitive as most other aspects of life and the foreign university place another score on the top level of the competition board. The pressure to succeed increasingly makes the life of the young in Bombay an endless round of examinations and tutors, but the arcane methods and politically in correct attitudes produce demonstrable professional and intellectual excellence.

Dining in an art deco apartment block or the dining room of an Edwardian club surrounded by aging polymaths, the people who formed independent India and now despair of her future as a united country, the past intellectual wealth of this city is elegantly on show. These are the people who benefited from the best of the old classical Indo-British education, studded with the hereditary jewels of Indian history and culture and sharpened by years of legal and political training. There are few people now in any country with this breadth of knowledge and experience as well as the continuing intellectual curiosity to look beyond the frilly trimmings of modern living to the horrendous obstacles but also bright possibilities of the future.

Their descendants, the students of today also look towards the future, a future of scientific innovations and wealth creation and travel but with little space or vocation for the public service of their grandfathers to community, city and country. As the hugely successful Indian diaspora spreads, who amongst these multi-talented young people will stay home or return from a lucrative career abroad to untangle the cat's cradle of modern skills, history, political rivalry, religious differences, corruption and extreme poverty in nuclear age India?

To expatriate eyes Bombay has all her multitude of wares on show, both at the heights and the depths of existence. The space created by each individual may be responsible for the ability of people to coexist in so proscribed an area of land. Affluence and poverty sit side by side and the poor do not attack the rich, only aspire to their wealth. Religious extremes exist of course and flare horrifically on occasion. By and large, in spite of extreme views expressed as volubly over smart dinner tables in Malabar Hill as in mosques and temples, Moslem, Hindu and Christian muddle through together and get on with their own daily lives and rituals.

India is far more resilient to the shocks and horrors gasped at in northern countries. The daily papers offer 'minor incidents', dozens dead; in the North a cause for mass mourning, government enquiries and national despondency. In Bombay a train crash or even a bomb does not stop the fatalistic rhythm of life. Expatriate companies and financial institutions are welcomed with open arms albeit dressed in red tape. Foreign exchange through foreign companies and tourism is encouraged as a key to prosperity.

Expatriate managers and staff are hardly required; the home-grown excellence needs to be used if it is to add to the future well-being of the city and not to be tempted overseas by greater rewards. All the components for a smooth running triumphant machine seem available, but the mechanism still lacks a masterplan and a key.

To dream of opportunity and the future in a city built on hope and aspiration is nothing new. Maybe it is a pipedream indeed to imagine that the jammed machine of Bombay could wind itself up again and be a leader in the continuing struggle for India to take her proper place at the international table, but this deep pool of diverse gifts should not be unused. The focus on the individual in the city has prevented the worst of the community rending problems in other parts of the country, but the individual, buried in his own vested interests, equally is not providing the cohesion necessary for the whole city to forge a spearhead for the future. Individual excellence encompasses all areas and all levels of professional life; there is an ambitious and growing middle class, but some balance of unself-interested public-service needs to be regenerated. Bombay has been cannibalized and reborn throughout her history and now seems capable of reinventing herself again using her inherent wealth of manpower and skills if the will can only be found.

Looking fondly at Bombay from a distance, there are so many gems to catch the eye, so many bright strands to untangle and so much grime and pain at the base. The poverty of Dharavi or villages all over India will not go away but a balanced and united modern country with proper processes in place for change and a role in world affairs will allow additional prosperity to filter down to the foundations on which it is built. The individual, the successful entrepreneur needs to revert to his traditional family values and transfer them to the macro family of the city.

Loyalty and support, duty and responsibility, pillars of Indian family life were also keystones of past public life and service in India. Such family values in the North are paid little more than lip-service but, where there is relatively strong and incorrupt government, similar social values are popularly accepted for the perceivable common good. Bombay may still be the city of gold but the mine is unsound and nuggets are being trodden into the earth by the rush of individual prospectors. Responsible and even-handed leadership must create a cohesive team to rebuild the structure and tap the deepest veins for the benefit of all.

A long life

NUVART PARSEGHIAN MEHTA

HEREWITH begins the second half of the narrator's life, in the humble service of Uncle Sam. What a jump from the city of skyscrapers to a good sized metropolis surrounded by water and being December, cool and comfortable. And what perks. I was lodged in a comfortable bedroom-sitting unit at the Oxford University Press building in Colaba. My hosts were a German couple, the Shaffers who were to become faithful friends. For the first time I was exposed to servants as an adult. A car picked me up and delivered me after office hours. The USIS office was at Adelphi, Churchgate, in an old-fashioned building. Eventually we moved to The International, next door, and many years later USIS on New Marine Lines became a permanent centre to spread the good word about American culture, study opportunities and ways of making the world shrink a bit.

I hardly caught my breath in my new environment when I was invited, to be precise on 22nd January 1953, to a cocktail party in one of the charming bungalows of New Marine lines. Among the guests was a dapper middle aged man with whom I danced. At the end of the party, he offered to take me home.

When we left in his little Austin, he was anxious to show me the city from the Malabar Hill heights (considered the classic approach). When he finally left me at my door, I did not have an inkling of how the encounter would change my life. For a gregarious person, my job was made to order, meeting not only Tom, Dick and Harry but academics, artists, and the general culture-vulture types! Each day was a challenge to serve the spirit of this American programme and on top of it to be paid for it! Of course there were times for rigorous self-restraint, not to blow up at unreasonable requests and attitudes but you learn soon if you want to keep your job.

We old timers refer to the 'golden fifties' when reminiscing of the social and cultural life we led in Bombay. It was gracious and perhaps conservative, as the present generation would think. We did not use the current (in the nineties) lingo of glitterati, literati (add illiterati!) for the genuine article was there in the personalities of very literate and creative men and women. The centre pieces of the fifties were the Taj Mahal Hotel and the Society Room at the Ambassador Hotel, not counting gracious private homes in the hills and Marine Lines. Lunch at the Society Room was a ritual, presided over by the genial host, Jack Voyantis. Now that I think of him, he was very much in the mould of Aristotle Onassis, Greek like him, if only physically. Food was excellent, atmosphere very high thinking assisted by liquid refreshments. The pianist gave us provocative music, no discos, thank you. Jack and I, both of Near East origin, exchanged recipes and more than once he supplied me with special ingredients flown in from Greece.

And conversation? It could not be dull with such luminaries as Frank Moraes, editor of *The Times of India*, soft spoken and of few words but a treat to listen to. Shawn Mandy, editor of *The Illustrated Weekly*, the Irishman of the twinkling blue eyes and naughty humour; impish Laxman, the cartoonist – the list can be a long one but years have slowed memory.

In the five years of my USIS assignment, the cultural scene was very active and very classy. The legendary Marian Anderson was among the first to perform as was Leontine Price, at the time a young unknown singer who attained international repute. I remember putting 500 chairs in the Taj Ballroom for a concert as there was at that time no large hall even for a few hundred persons. For Marian Anderson a local orchestra was put together by the western music aficionado, Vere da Silva. Rudolf Serkin was next. Then Martha Graham and her troupe, not to mention the Minneapolis Symphony Orchestra with Anton Dorati and then the San Francisco Ballet. Those were the days for western classical programmes.

Along with my work, something was brewing on the romantic front – the protagonist being the Parsi gentleman who had showed me the Bombay skyline on 22nd January 1953. It was too early to forecast the romantic future because of family obligations on my part and restrictions in the foreign service rules. The latter would change drastically with women's lib.

Somewhere along this time, 1954, the greatest and most thrilling event was my reunion with my brother in Melbourne – over 12,000 miles by air. Three decades had gone by since we had been together. For the first day he was like a handsome boy friend until we caught up our childhood threads again. Although we had both developed differently, me international, he very faithful to his Armenian roots, we got along very well. He had launched a project to establish an Armenian Apostolic Church in Melbourne.

Just as you see in the movies, there was a mistake in arrival time and after all kinds of palpitation for the great reunion, he was not there to meet me. When we finally did, his first comment was 'My, how you have grown!' Indeed, I was 14 when my father left us and took him along, and 44 when we met again.

After returning to Bombay from home leave for a second term in 1955, serious thought had to be given about the future as there was no doubt that a third term would not be granted. 1957 was a decisive year. Both of us, confirmed bachelors and already middle aged, took the plunge and decided on marriage. A request for permission, accompanied by a letter of resignation went to Washington headquarters. The letter of resignation was accepted: That was it.

We announced our official engagement on June 13th (considered my lucky day since my American citizenship was granted on 13th November 1947). We arranged to have the engagement party in the USIS offices where my Indian and American colleagues and I had worked together very happily for five years.

There was a bit of hue and cry from my family, devout Armenian Christians. They remembered the religious wars of the fifth century in Iran. Zoroastrians, the faith of my husband to be, and Armenians had clashed in the fifth century when the former tried to convert by the sword. The enemy was 220,000 strong. Armenians mustered 66,000 soldiers. The general, Vartan, in spite of a small army, saved the faith. To this day he is honoured as a saint, in the month of February. The irony, historically, of this event is that about two centuries later these same Zoroastrians fled Iran when the Muslims invaded the country. That is when the Parsis landed on the western coast of India. And this is the minuscule minority which has done so much for the general progress of India.

To come back to happier events and to add that Nari's family's attitude was impeccable, Uncle Sam did not get his money's worth in the next six months as I plunged into preparations for the big event. There was much discussion on the date. Parsis have imbibed Hindu concepts such as position of stars, auspicious days and what not. We also had to consider the inconvenience to golfing friends if our big event was to take place on a weekend.

One comment still makes me laugh. When we announced December 21st as the wedding day to the wife of the Consul General, a very proper and dignified lady, she exclaimed: 'Oh my, Nuvart, that is the longest night of the year!' True, the solstice, as June 21st is the longest day of the year.

Nari and his family graciously agreed that in addition to the civil marriage, I could have a religious service. But where? I started shopping for a church. My Armenian church said yes, but first we must baptize him. I said nothing doing. The Church of England said the bishop would only bless the rings. And wonder of wonders, the Wesley Church in Colaba said since one member is a Christian, a full ceremony could be held. Once this knotty problem was solved, we plunged into much socializing and getting details worked out. I dashed to beat import restrictions to purchase pale pink Chantilly lace. It was stored away in a friend's air conditioned bedroom to protect it from the tropical weather. The dress turned out well but the petticoat was so stiff, I did not sit down once.

In spite of partying, I had been swimming and playing badminton to keep some semblance of a waistline and to obey my volatile Italian dressmaker's instructions 'Hold it in, pull it in.' 'But Madame Bussi I can't breathe.' 'I don't care, you must look right on that day' – all this in priceless Italian English. I did not care for a bouquet, as I had always cherished my grandmother's prayerbook. It was covered with dull satin, two gladioli buds and my family heirloom, a jewelled butterfly pin. There was a minor crisis before I left for church when we discovered that I had given my keys to Nari earlier who was already at church and I could not get to my engagement ring. That solved, the next contretemps in my mounting excitement, I made Nari take the wrong ring, so I could not push his all the way down when my turn came. But fortunately a prayer followed during the ceremony and we quietly changed our rings.

The reception was held at a maharajah's palace which eventually became Lincoln House, the home of the American Consulate General. By Indian standards, it was a very small reception, only 300. The pink cake was catered by Bombellis, a Swiss old-timer. The Indian gift giving is a welcome change from bits of odds and ends – cash. What was collected took care of our honeymoon and then some.

Before we left for our honeymoon the next day, my special passport had to be changed to an ordinary one by an officer on special duty for me on a Sunday.

Having been a spinster for so long, it took time for me to refer to Nari as my husband. I practised during the trip to the Nilgiris: Ooty at 7500 feet, at a farmhouse in the slopping downs, still a British Raj mellow atmosphere. When we visited again some years later, the whole area was ugly and commercialized. This has been happening in all of India, and Bombay is a prime example of what I mean. Our romantic sea shore has been reclaimed and skyscrapers vie with each other for height and dullness. The private homes, bungalows, in tree shaded lanes, have been replaced by commercial establishments. Along with the physical change, what about the leadership? How tall they walked, Nehru, Sardar Patel, Radhakrishnan, Zakir Husain, men of learning, morality, dedication. And now? Instead of being statesmen, to be a politician now is a 'profession', like being an engineer or a doctor, to make a living out of it. Patriots? They are only legends now. For one who has lived here for half her life, it's to have witnessed a dream, now lost.

I was doing all housekeeping chores on our return to our Bombay home. I can well see the grins on all faces when I am mourning that I have no servant! Shopping in Bombay means that one brings a chicken home from the market practically intact, except for a slit throat. Fish comes with all scales and bones on. The biggest struggle at the time, however, was how to make poached eggs which Nari liked for breakfast. It is tricky. The second struggle was to find enough room for Nari's 'junk'. If they say women collect, I know how it is exaggerated. Pipes galore, hooks and buttons, cigar boxes, wall calendars, aeroplane models, torchlights – a veritable thieves market.

In mid 1959 I became a working woman again. The Fulbright Foundation in Delhi had opened a regional Bombay office and I was asked to take charge of it. Fortune was smiling extra for the Department of State at this time wanted to borrow me for a period of three months to handle a project under the President's cultural programme. Inasmuch as I had never been a TV enthusiast, I had never heard of Red Alexander's Dance Jubilee. But I was in a dilemma. My mother had come from Istanbul to live with us; she was recuperating from an illness. As Nari was to handle travel arrangements and go around the country ahead of time, it meant mother was to be alone. Gutsy woman that she was, she told us to go ahead. I flew to Teheran to get acquainted with the troupe. While struggling with artistic temperaments, I enjoyed the compensations; caviar (black not red) and services in the Armenian Church, complete with cymbals and musical bells.

I returned to Bombay with ten dancers, five musicians, one singer and five stage crew. They performed 38 times all over the country. Each move needed one chartered plane for the equipment and one for the personnel. Nari's buddies were quite envious since the personnel included three young blondes, one gorgeous Mexican and some of the time I was not on the trip! On this particular project I discovered that among his many virtues, my husband was a very efficient businessman.

My memories of a successful tour are marred by tragic ones. Mother attended one of the shows but while going down the steps she fell and broke her hip. But we were blessed by the quality of the doctors and nurses. Dr. Rani, the eye doctor, was a handsome tall Parsi who had studied in England. Dr. Amson, a German refugee, a saint who walks the earth – one of those unusual doctors who phones in for a report on the patient if one has failed to phone him!

In spite of all the loving care, I lost my mother in May 1960. To honour her wishes, we arranged to take her remains to Istanbul to be buried next to her parents. As we were to board the plane, it was announced that the Istanbul airport was closed due to a coup. Deep in sorrow, we returned to the city and buried her in the Armenian cemetery which dates back to the 18th century. The Fort area is the old stamping ground of those who founded the city. The Armenian Church was founded in 1796, a few lanes away from Bruce Street, the area commonly referred to as the Tata headquarters. The cemetery, however, is in the far suburbs, Wadala.

To anticipate, let me narrate that my mother's wishes were honoured some 20 years later when her remains were, accompanied by me, flown to Istanbul. Incredible as it may sound in modern times, the airlines lost the box containing her remains and sent it to cargo in New York. For six weeks we had no news. To lighten the poignancy of our anxiety, we resorted to humour and said mother always enjoyed travelling. Eventually the box was found and interred next to her parents in Istanbul.

1962 was the year when India had a border confrontation with China. When we returned from one of our periodic trips, the barrage of patriotism engulfed us. We read daily lists of cash and gold donations for the defence fund. 'Ornaments and Armaments, give generously to the National Defence Fund', 'give India your blood, gold and work – she needs it now', 'talk less, work more', I was particularly happy with the Air India cartoon at a main Bombay thoroughfare. It showed a boyish Kennedy and a dignified Macmillan being profusely garlanded by a delegation of two men and two women, a non-vegetarian rolly-polly Parsi woman, a streamlined Hindu woman, a skinny Congressman and a grinning Sikh, saying in union 'Bless you both.'

After the ceasefire, we faced uncertainty, politically and militarily. No uncertainty, however, about the welfare of the jawan, the simple, semi-literate but sturdy soldier is the Man of the Year. Nothing is too good for him: society ladies purl one, knit two at their bridge tables, in between deals. Two thousand booths sprung up in the city, to 'vote for victory' – each vote costing one local unit, a rupee.

Whether as a result of the political and military situation I don't know, but new import restrictions were announced. I don't know the difference between ball bearings and bolt nuts, but I do know the difference between White Horse and Black Knight. My connoisseur husband insists that if you add a peg of sherry to Black Knight, the local brand, it improves. Foreign cars, iceboxes, electric appliances were on their way to the museum. Our newly acquired General Electric icebox was enthroned in our Americanized kitchen, as precious to me as a walky talky doll to a Fiji child.

Again USIS removed my ennui after coming down to earth from spiritual heights. NASA sent an educational venture to India

– a space-mobile van, gaily decorated with American and Indian flags, with realistic models of Titan, Explorer, Echo, Mercury, etc. I who have flunked every science course, had to understand all this. The team consisted of an American lecturer, three Indian scientists, two drivers and me, the mother hen.

Variety being the spice of life was not a banal expression in my life. From space, I began to swing to jazz, when Duke Ellington and his orchestra came to Bombay, again under the USIS sponsorship. Again I had to pretend – to be a jazz buff. At the time I had not realized that Indians were crazy about jazz. Ticket lines formed in the night, just like at the Met, the only difference being that one does not shiver waiting in line during the night and we can send servants to keep our place in the line, both considerable advantages.

The biggest administrative problem was to get the group to keep to the schedule, all prima donnas. Each member needed an attendant to insure appearance at functions, even at concerts. One would collect five, go after the next five, and return to discover that the first five had disappeared. Concerts were sellouts, and held in an outdoor theatre, seating 3000. October is a dry month in Bombay, but it had been raining. We consulted the weather bureau, offered prayers to all the gods of the pantheon, kept all kinds of charms around. Result: dry days and a first class downpour 10 minutes after the last concert!

On our reasonably frantic calendar, pretty good for quite an elderly couple, was the visit of the Los Angeles Symphony Orchestra, and its Bombay born conductor, Zubin Mehta. We have basked temporarily in reflected glory. Whether in the States or in Europe, we were always asked if we were related. There are some 30 pages of Mehtas in the telephone directory. The closest 'relationship' was the fact that my husband and Zubin's father sat next to each other in college, doubtless an alphabetic convenience! At another time when attending Zubin's Lucerne festival, we went backstage to meet him. When we gave our name to his secretary, with a sneer, she said 'Really?' Without a sneer we answered 'Yes, really, Mehta.' All male Parsi children, born during his visit in India, in November, were named Zubin; but not 'Zuby baby' bestowed on him by American admirers, if we were to believe press stories. Among this great orchestra of 110 musicians, I proudly spotted one Armenian, the assistant concertmaster.

One night we came home and found a car parked in the space reserved for us. It was a neighbour's car, the chauffeur dead drunk, giggling, and a dead body in the back seat. He had knocked down the man, cruised around at a loss what to do and eventually landed in our compound. At this time Bombay was supposed to be a strictly dry city!

Major and minor events in our daily lives in Bombay interested and amused me. One day in September I was a full-fledged Christian in the morning and a 'Hindu' in the afternoon. Our car was piled with pilgrims to St. Mary's Cathedral for its feast day: two Americans, one Parsi, one Roman Catholic and one Hindu. In the evening, Rauji, our Hindu servant and I witnessed a Ganapati immersion, the half-man, half-elephant god who removes obstacles. Clay models are worshipped for 10 days and then immersed in the sea with much pomp and circumstance.

Although we have been blessed with faithful and uncomplaining servants, at one ladies luncheon for 10, there were two vegetarians but one of them did not eat eggs on that particular day, one was a Muslim who did not eat pork (therefore two quiche lorraines, one without bacon) the rest meat eaters but no veal! But no complaints from our good servants.

My daily laughs came free from the matrimonial ads in our morning paper. Here is one: 'Wanted intelligent bridge for twenty-five years tall (174 cms) handsome, enthusiastic, accomplished, cultured world travelled professor and consulting engineer with Doctor of Science (USA) and British education with over Rs 15000 per month income. Girl must be very beautiful over 160 cms, tall with pretty figure with good nature and habits. Hindi speaking from a good sociable family between 21-24 years; slim, about 50 kg, minimum education BA or BBS, cultured, loving, mature and would like to continue her education in USA for the next two years. No bars or other requirements. Early marriage. Please send full details in confidence to box 28106.' Any takers?

As if this ad was not enough to saturate us, there was a delicious language mix-up when a dear Swiss friend who knows three other languages fluently, wrote to us 'I must have caught something which the stomach did not very much appreciate. On the way I collapsed and I was away for about five minutes.' Soon after we found the following note from Luis, our cook 'Mr. Natesan bring package for Sahib. Not giving to servant. Jesus Christ.'

The high of the year was a birth: the import of our New York car. Nari says it was like having a baby, inasmuch as it took nine months of work, uncertainty, plus two trips to Delhi, mountains of paper work and 110% duty. We garlanded this new arrival, a 1962 Mercury Comet, in the Indian traditional way, and for added measure, stuck on a Near Eastern charm 'a blue eye bead', a 'nazaar'. In the midst of small domestic cars, it really looks and acts like a Cadillac. Up to now I had to be content to be wife two, golf being one. Now I am third. If I cough all night, Nari says take some syrup, but should the car sneeze, ah…!

A rebel with many causes

JEHANGIR SABAVALA

IT is intimidating to write a celebratory article about a parent, alas dead now for over three decades. Whilst alive, to use a cliché, so much water flowed under the bridge – currents and cross-currents, sparkle and murk, and if one is to be honest, of like and dislike! The assignment, in cold black and white, is a disturbing one.

And yet if one does not comply, disloyalty and guilt add their unpleasant quota to the roiling waters. Memory haunts me vividly, but the person has vanished to be reborn, perhaps to a calm, and not to a restless, stormy life. A life left so incomplete.

I speak of mother, widely known by her moniker 'Bapsey'. Christened Meherbai, she was the third and youngest child born to Sir Cowasji Jehangir (1st Bart) and Lady Dhunbai Cowasji Jehangir, in Bombay in 1892.

The Raj rode astride the Indian Empire – and she was a Parsee Victorian. Born to an illustrious and wealthy Zoroastrian family, which was expanding its business interests (cotton mills, real estate, money lending) and consolidating its fortune, it was also learning how to use its wealth wisely and well, through benefaction and philanthropy, thus amply rewarding the city for all that the latter had given to it.

The tradition of charity started with Bapsey's ancestor, her grandfather, the 1st Sir Cowasji Jehangir (KCIE) and was carried on into her day by her own extended efforts. The family endowed Bombay with schools, hospitals, the University Convocation Hall, the Elphinstone College, the Jehangir Art Gallery, the Cowasji Jehangir Public Hall, now the National Gallery of Modern Art – just to mention a few of the memorable landmarks that recall its munificence.

A late child, she was indulged by her parents. Charming pictures exist of Bapsey being cradled between her brother (the 2nd Bart) and her much older, sari-clad sister, Cooverbai. The enchanting early photograph, hand-tinted and reproduced on porcelain, is from Vienna, which city excelled in romantic representation, and catered to a rich international clientele. Later pictures in my possession are of a slim, winsome girl-child – demurely bonneted with bows and plumes, all in white. This was Bapsey at the age of seven, photographed in London around the turn of the 20th century.

Not the slightest hint exists of the maverick, the remarkable woman that was to emerge from this chrysalis. Bapsey in an interview with R.K. of the *Current* in the early '50s had this to say – 'I was born dead, and was a very delicate child, but one that survived, and later, began to look like a ravishing doll.'

Subsequent photographs began to reveal the incipient strength and strong-willed traits that became her hallmark. Bapsey at around 18 – dressed as a Kashmiri 'belle', in a house boat, in traditional headgear, dripping ethnic jewellery. The stance is already bold, the face handsome, portents of the future clearly defined.

As a pre-adolescent, she enjoyed nothing more than dressing up and playing roles. A passion for acting and drama was ingrained in her. Her favourite part was to emulate Lady Lawrence Jenkins, the wife of the then Chief Justice of Bombay Presidency.

Bapsey had the upbringing of an emancipated Indo-Victorian, given the typical Parsi upper class setting to which she belonged. Schooling was more private than public. There were the 'Mehtaji's' to oversee Gujarati, writing, and her calculation skills. And there were English governesses to teach her the language, the arts, and correct etiquette – all a part of her curriculum. A love of music and the theatre was induced under the tutelage of a Miss Schmuck (Bapsey became a good amateur pianist, and the theatre was a consuming passion), and as a young person she was an accomplished horsewoman.

It was one of her governesses, a Miss Dicky, who used to throw the little bundle of joy up into the air, saying 'Babsy Wabsy darling baby' and that is how her name Bapsey was coined, to remain with her for all of her life. The sedate 'Meherbai' got left behind, and was relegated to official and legal usage only.

I remember travelling with mother as a boy, always an exciting happening. I especially enjoyed being taken to the theatre, the more so as she had a penchant for demanding entrance to the dressing-rooms of famous stars. She inevitably got her way. Dressed resplendently in flamboyant sarees, and ornately jewelled, a young son in tow – she was indeed a rare sight in the London and Paris of 75 years ago.

I recall the gracious Dame Sybil Thorndyke and Emyln Williams, performing in 'The Corn is Green'. And in New York, the glamorous Tallulah Bankhead, the lead in 'The Little Foxes'. Not only did we barge into the latter's dressing-room, but after the performance, Tallulah escorted us home, in her enormous, chauffeured limousine. Do you wonder that I, all of 17, was totally star-struck? John Gielgud during a visit to Bombay was left speechless when mother invited him to our home, known as 'Aewan-e-Rafiyat', on Malabar Hill. Her command – 'Come and have lunch with me, my house is a symphony in stone!' He did, and wrote about it in his autobiography.

By the way, to let you in on a secret, her imagined name in 'lights' was Zita Lasa. Alas, never used, never marqueed! But she did become well-known on the local amateur stage of the Bombay of those days. She also produced and directed one of the first early films of the '20s, entitled *Darkness into Light*, in which she starred as the ill-fated heroine.

Later came several theatre productions directed and produced by her. Dil-Pazir, which was designed by *the* Karl Khandalawalla (lawyer, scholar, author of the LKA series on Indian art), premiered at the old Capitol Theatre. He conceived marvellous living cameos reconstructed from ancient and modern Indian paintings. And again in 1940, *Fantasy in a Mediaeval Indian Street* was directed by Bapsey and scripted by Karl.

She was considered a 'bombshell for orthodoxy'. She appeared on the stage to assert the right of the Parsi woman to act with members of the opposite sex, just when a controversy was raging in the newspapers on the subject.

Resisting all attempts at a good alliance, Bapsey married at 26, late for her time, and against her parents' wishes. My father Ardeshir Pestonjee Sabavala, was a qualified barrister from the Inns of Court, London, young and good-looking but with no means worth mentioning. He met her there, where she was travelling with her parents. He was well-educated and stemmed from good 'Surat stock'. She was a lovely heiress. Bapsey married my father, left her luxurious ancestral home, to set up house as an ordinary housewife – which ambition was alas short-lived. They had two children, myself and my older brother Shahrookh. Soon enough the young husband was lured into Sir Cowasji's patriarchal mansion. He joined the family business and sadly, gave up law altogether.

The marriage was fraught from the start. But following the mores of the times, it dragged on for several long years, till she eventually divorced my father in the mid '40s. It was one of the early, much publicized, Bombay divorce cases. Somewhere along the line, I suspect, mother enjoyed the high drama and sensationalism of it all. Discretion was not one of her virtues. She was never one to allow the dust to be quietly swept under the carpet. Both my parents suffered the consequences of a traumatic break-up, as indeed did we, their children.

Now minus husband, and with the offspring old enough to fend for themselves, Bapsey was once again a free woman. The encumbrances of hearth and home were shed, behind her once and for all.

Despite the social taboos, the tight reins of male domination, she became what would, in the previous generation, have been called a suffragette. Rebellious, self-willed, uncompromising, she ran afoul of society. She was never the elegant, accomplished hostess that her world wanted and expected her to be.

Bapsey was born at the wrong time, in the wrong place, when women of her station were not trained for a profession. Had she been born today, she would have undoubtedly excelled – as an activist, a feminist, and been trained as a social worker, harnessing all that surplus energy in a disciplined manner.

It was as early as 1920 that Bapsey organized her first charity venture for the victims of the Jallianwalla Bagh massacre. As her personal life ran aground with her parents and her husband, she plunged deeper into a stream of activities.

In the early days she supported Ardeshir strongly in his political ambitions. He stood for several municipal elections and later political ones. Bapsey went all out, canvassing for him, from house to house, street to street, inspite of the growing divide between them. But, it was only after the divorce that she was free to take to social work seriously – full time. The upliftment of the poor and the needy was a cause close to her heart.

Bapsey was responsible for establishing the first *Swabal* (self-help) store in Colaba, the only one of its kind in the city then. Its purpose was to prevent young, unqualified Parsi males from merely loafing, and to give them a feel of the dignity of labour. The store was to serve the needs of everyday lives. There was instant opposition to the scheme from both sexes, especially from men, who felt it demeaning to undertake such work. So, to set an example, it was Bapsey herself who swept the floors of the shop clean. Subsequently, a 'Swabal' chain was established in Bombay, successfully.

The Haji Ali Sonavala Andhakashi Ashram for the blind was an early centre that gave physical succour and medical aid to the unseeing, irrespective of caste or creed. Bapsey worked tirelessly to make this early venture work. Eventually in 1938, a functioning home in Andheri was established, inaugurated by Lady Dhunbai, her mother, and in the presence of Lady Blackwell, the wife of the Chief Justice of Bombay.

Bapsey was a staunch Indian, also a staunch Zoroastrian. But this did not prevent her from opening wide the doors of her home to all religions. Every year, on Gandhiji's birthday, she held an ecumenical evening, when scholars and devotees of every faith addressed the audience and exchanged their views. Incidentally, the nuns of St. Catherine's Home still remember her warmly, for the enormous support she gave to this Christian Mission house.

The charity fetes – for schools, hospitals, for the sick and the maimed, that she organized were legion, and she collected funds for them almost single-handedly. To the corporate sector, mother was a nightmare. She was ever present, cajoling, demanding of businessmen that they part with their shekels for one of her causes. She had a will of iron and a way with her, and though maddened by her, the city respected her – inspite of the growing eccentricities and brusqueness of manner. I should know, for I grew up amidst this welter of activity and confusion.

Let me enumerate a few of the extravaganzas which she so ably organized. 'Help our Hospitals', a week-long fete at the Azad Maidan. The Four Charities Prize Calendar Scheme – this for the Viceroy's War Fund/the Relief of the Blind/Beggar Uplift/and Parsi Industrial and Agricultural Settlements. The Dil-Pazir Fete. The Punjab Refugee Ball (also known as the Blanket Ball) in 1948. The Bijapur Relief Fund, 1973. And always, till she died, she gave her full support to the Matheran Social Welfare Scheme. Matheran – with which hill station she had a deep and abiding love affair – was her second home and refuge.

Her love of animals was another facet of her personality. It made her espouse many projects devoted to their wellbeing. It also accounted for the menagerie with which we grew up – of dogs, cats, birds, a deer, and even a pet porky. In the days when we lived in Europe, this exotic lady, with her entourage of children, governesses, servants, and pets, was a sight not to be easily effaced. Bombaites of the day will not forget how she made a horse climb the famous staircase of the Taj Mahal Hotel to participate in an animal cabaret.

No mention of Bapsey can ever be complete without referring to her passion for dolls. She had no attraction whatsoever for the conventional cuddly doll. As with everything else she created a fantasy world of these 'inanimate creatures' and surrounded herself with them. Every nook and corner of her bedroom was inhabited by them – in cloth, clay, celluloid, china – and the rounder they were the better. Japan was particularly strongly represented in her collection. But it was the 'Cupie' doll that had pride of place in her heart. A period piece, which I doubt exists any more, with its coy pertness, mischievous eyes, lipsticked smile, an oversized neon-coloured bow – worn as a dog collar. When Bapsey was invited out to friends, she took along with her one of the favourites of the day as a co-guest. I have always thought of this as extraordinary behaviour, which in today's world would attract psychological interpretation. It became a badge, an accepted Bapsey eccentricity, a harmless amusing one. But the deeper malaise escaped the attention of most people – and this is quite clear in retrospect.

Bapsey knew no fear. The fact that she was a woman, or her own privileged and sheltered background, never daunted her. She wished to be accepted as she was. I remember the fright and consternation we felt when she collected people off the street – beggars, the sick and the sorry – and packed them into the car, to be delivered to the right quarters. The sensibilities of others was not her forte, and was something that she never bothered herself with. It was incredible and wonderful, of course, but there were at times, elements of bravado and ruthlessness in her missions of mercy.

All of this will perhaps explain why mother was so widely known in Bombay and elsewhere. The legend spread and several appellations were attached to her name. I give you a sampling – by turn cruel and kind – 'Bapsey – the married widow'/'the indefatigable institution'/'Queen Elizabeth-I, minus the lovers'/'the professional beggar for lost causes'/'a God-send to Bombay'/and 'Gypsy Queen', which was Sir Joseph Kay's favourite name for her.

Mother was at her ease with the dignitaries and the politicians of her day. Being completely apolitical herself she was trusted by all as the city's crusader. The erstwhile British governors and their wives were on friendly terms with her not only because of her family background, but more so because of her formidable reputation for social work, for which she was awarded the Kaiser-I-Hind medal. As were people of the stature of Kanhialal Munshi, S.K. Patil and Morarji Desai. A special friend was India's Nightingale, Sarojini Naidu, who used to visit our home when I was a boy. That mother was capable of naming one of her menagerie after a politician may well have been so, but I cannot vouch for this – as memories fade.

But the ravages of time, unhappiness, and I suspect, an unrequited need of companionship – for which neither husband, children, lover, vocation, ever qualified. All of this took its toll, and Bapsey very sadly slid into an isolated world of her own – wilful to the end, but tired and very lonely. Her good looks and dramatic charisma, the flash and the fire, had gone. And I saw a remarkable person disintegrate in front of my eyes.

A woman who had lived by her own rules, the way she had wanted to, who did not care for pomp or glory. An apocryphal anecdote about her tells of how she laughingly asked of a government official, who had come for preliminary inquiries about a 'Padma Shri Award' to be given to her. 'What kind of a toy is this Padma Shri?'

It was the well-known R.K. Karanjia, the editor of *Blitz*, who in 1970 remembered that it was the 'great little lady' who came to the rescue of B.G. Horniman – famed Irish journalist, who had fought and suffered for India's freedom – by collecting a purse of Rs 50,000 and even paying his medical bills and rent, when he fell upon bad days.

She was candid and forthright to a fault. I remember an incident that did the rounds of Bombay society. Mother was on one of her habitual missions, and this time she was to meet the wife of one of Bombay's top industrialists – a charming woman, but a complete waffler, who busied herself lending a helping hand, somewhat vaguely. The good lady was rambling on pleasantly, when suddenly Bapsey boomed – 'Cut the cackle, is it a yes or a no?' A gasp and tears flowed.

Bapsey was especially gifted with the younger generation. An able organizer, she enjoyed arranging games, theatricals, parties, with verve and originality. Even the food was somehow different, albeit whimsical, but charmingly decorated, with a personal flair. As an aside, she became a vegetarian in late life, out of conviction. As she loved dressing up she frequently gave fancy dress parties, at one of which she appeared as the Air India Maharaja.

Mother enjoyed the company of the young, being young at heart herself. And they on their part, were drawn to her non-conformism – as to a magnet.

And I end on a well-merited eulogy. 'No cause or mission... was too small or insignificant, or out of the way for her... To call Bapsey a social-worker or philanthropist would be an insult to her prodigious, titanic passion for serving the poor and the faltering.'

Runaway: A chronicle of metropolitan transience

SUKETU MEHTA

I HAVE been on the lookout for a driver after the last one decamped with the money I foolishly advanced him. I begin to notice a taxidriver who always has his cab waiting in the compound of my building, Dariya Mahal, by seven in the morning. His taxi is always clean smelling, with freshly lit agarbattis in front of the shrine over the dashboard, and the driver is always polite, with sandalwood paste on his forehead from his morning puja.

Early one morning, stepping out of Dariya Mahal to go to my office in Bandra, I find his taxi waiting outside and get into conversation with him. His name is Ramesh, and when he learns that I'm writing a book, he says, 'I can't read or write. If I could I would write such a story for you.' He knows every lane of the city, knows where all the crime is. He has seen the public running from a police encounter, seen four men pull out a rickshawallah and stab him to death. He knows the brothel opposite Simla House, and know of another one in Ashoka Apartments next to Petit Hall, where good-looking girls from the village are brought and fed till they look nice, and sold for up to 50,000 a night. 'I can't write, otherwise I could write you such a story.' His fate in life was decided by five rupees worth of coffee.

When the taxi passes Haji Ali he touches his eyes and kisses his fingers 'for Haji Ali Baba.' There isn't a single Muslim in his village – they have another village all to themselves – but Ramesh says, 'I believe in Allah, and also in Bhagwan. It is the same.'

He wants me to hire him, but not as a driver. 'Will your book have pictures? I will take pictures. You can give me a camera, and whenever I come upon a scene I'll take a picture of it for you. I drive a taxi all day, and I see scenes all the time, amazing scenes. People won't mind my taking a picture because I drive a taxi.' He will take pictures of accident scenes, stabbing scenes, crowd scenes. I ask him to come to my office to talk it over. And so he appears in Bandra, one Sunday afternoon, and I make tea for him. I would not have been able to do this – make tea for a driver and serve him, stirring the sugar for him – if I'd grown up and stayed in Bombay. I went abroad and lost a sense of caste.

We talk all day; at lunchtime I give him money to go to the Lucky restaurant for some biryani. I want to eat my lunch and check my e-mail and I expect he'll be gone for an hour or two. But he comes back in half an hour eager to continue his life-story. He had been growing up in Dariya Mahal around the same time I had, but he had been growing up in the garages, the servants' quarters. When he mentions the landmarks of his childhood – the school, the sea, the garden, the underground garages – I realize they are the same as mine, and he can fill me in on the details of the other world, of the servants, drivers, and cooks that co-inhabited our space without intersecting with our lives. When they did, the results were generally disastrous, for us and them.

He tells his story well, without elaboration, without excess adornment, leaning forward slightly, eager to get to the next plot point in his tumultuous life. I can write it down and relate it almost exactly as he is telling it to me, without my having to interpret or explain for him. It is a chronicle of metropolitan transience, of constant movement between the village and the city and abroad; and a life always under the threat of violence.

Ramesh Gowda is '32 or 33, I don't know definitely.' He is from the village of Kundur, about 40 kms outside of Mysore. There are 500 households in the village and of each family at least two people work in Bombay. They work as domestics, in small restaurants, as gardeners, in factories, as drivers and car-washers. Most of them live in Chembur, close to giant chemical factories. But Ramesh's family lived in a more upscale area: Nepean Sea Road. His father worked in Walshingham School – which my own sisters had both attended – and would come back to the village for a month every year or every two years and would bring from Bombay biscuits, soap, clothes, and his bad temper. He lived with a certain style in Bombay, and resented having to send money back to his family. After Ramesh's grandfather died, his father came back permanently and tormented his family; he couldn't find work, couldn't live well in the village.

Ramesh grew up hating school and loving trees. He was climbing a tamarind tree once, and the master caught him and beat him with a stick. He hit him back with a slate, and ran away. When his father came to know, 'he beat me a lot.' To avoid school, the boy would run into the fields and spend the days there. After a few days his father found out 'and beat me a lot again.' Again, for eight days, he hid behind his house. He would hide till the school let out, then join the other boys. This time, when his father found out, he lifted him by the hands and dashed him against the ground. Then he hit him on the head with a stick.

Ramesh shows me now, two decades later, the scar on his temple from the beating. 'He said I should die.' His mother and sisters thought that he would kill the boy, and they were wailing. Afterwards, he was taken out of school and sent to herd the cows and goats in the mountains around the village. His recounting of his cowherd days sounds like the tales of Krishna in Mathura. 'I would take them at nine in the morning, and bring them back at five-thirty. Eight to ten of us went up into the jungle. All day we would play pranks on each other. We would let each other's cattle into the sugarcane fields, where they would eat the cane and the farmer would tie up the cow. I would climb up into their coconut trees and drink the coconuts. They complained to my father.'

One day he drove the buffaloes into a river, and asked another boy to come into the water; he would teach him swimming. The boy came in, and began to drown. Ramesh shouted at him to hold a buffalo's tail; then Ramesh hit the buffalo, and the animal dragged the boy out of the water. But the other boys told Ramesh's father that his son had almost been the cause of the boy's death. His father then decided to send him away to Bombay. There wasn't much of a future for him in the village, anyway. That year the village had nothing to eat. The crops had failed and there was no work. The villagers took to going to the riverbank and picking a particular kind of grass, and cooking and eating it.

Ramesh was one of seven; five brothers and two sisters. One of his brothers was working as a domestic in Sagar Kunj, behind Dariya Mahal. His father wrote to him to send money for Ramesh's train passage. He didn't, and his father decided to sell ten goats for his passage. They took the goats 10 kilometres away to the market town, but none of the goats sold. He got mad; said that Ramesh was bringing him bad luck, and brought him back all the way to the village beating him. 'My father beat me again at home, and my mother was crying, saying he would kill me.'

His mother appealed to her nephew, who had come from Bombay. The nephew promised to take Ramesh back with him. Ramesh was very happy to be going to Bombay; he told everybody about it. He used to gape at the men coming back from the city: 'they were healthy, not thin like the villagers. They wore chappals; I used to stare at their chappals, since we didn't wear any. They would wear pants and shoes.' The village existed in a kind of timelessness. Ramesh had never seen a movie, he didn't know what it was. When a motorcycle came through town he would run after it for two kilometres, in wonderment.

When he was 10 years old, Ramesh was sent with his uncle and cousin to Bombay. They woke up at four on a Monday morning. His mother packed him two pairs of clothes, and food: yoghurt rice packed in *supari* leaves, and *wadas*. She had taught him: 'keep your hands inside the window in the train.' They walked the three kilometres into the city – there were no buses. Then they took a lorry to the train at Asikeri. Ramesh annoyed his cousin with his pranks on the train – pressing the taps, looking at the lights, staring at the vendors on the platforms. They changed for the Mahalaxmi Express at Miraj, and got off at Dadar, and took a taxi to Chembur.

On the ride, he opened the taxi door by mistake and his cousin hit him. They got to the slum of his uncle, who worked in a factory. Ramesh saw a bicycle outside; he got on it for a ride and crashed into some women gathering water, breaking their pots. They shouted at him, and he brought back the cycle and left it outside his uncle's home. Shortly after, it went missing; it had been confiscated by the women whose pots were broken. The uncle threw him out, and sent him to another uncle in Santacruz, who placed him as a house servant for a Gujarati family. They gave him nice things to eat: *chapatti* with *ghee*, sweet *dal*, fine rice. 'I loved this. I looked at the TV and saw people in it and wondered how the people got in there. I was told they got in there through current, but I didn't know what current was since our village had no current.'

One day his employer gave him five rupees and asked him to go to the market, and buy coffee. As he was walking by the station, he saw the local train coming. 'I stopped and stared at it. I found it strange – this huge train.' He was near the canteen, and saw people drinking cold drinks. Drawn in by thirst and the enticing sodas, he gave the canteen man the five rupees and he gave Ramesh a bottle of Fanta, and the change. 'I thought in five rupees I could buy the world.' Then a train came into the station. The boy got in the train, with all the rest of the public. The train stopped at Dadar, and he got off. He wandered around the station. It was three in the afternoon by this time, and he suddenly remembered the coffee, and was scared. He had spent one rupee and 40 paise; he was afraid to face his employer.

Ramesh thought he should run back to his village. 'There was another train waiting, and I got on it.'

That train went to Kalyan station, about an hour out of Bombay, and Ramesh got down. He didn't know where he was, he didn't know the language. He couldn't ask anyone how to get home, an address which he didn't know. He slept on the platform. The next day, he spent 60 paise on two wadas. A train pulled in, bound for Poona, and he got on it. Another train took him to Daun station. He ate some more, and his money finished. He kept taking more trains all around the West, for a week, till he got to Gundakkal. There he saw a boy begging below the train. Someone threw him fried rice and Ramesh watched him eating. He stood in front of a canteen. The owner asked Ramesh what he wanted, and he said food. He put the boy to work washing glasses, and then gave him something to eat. Another train came, which brought him back to Kalyan.

At Kalyan he met a deaf-mute man. There was a tree on the number six platform, and as Ramesh was sitting below it, the mute gestured to him. He was a beggar, and much older than Ramesh, at least 45. He had lived all his life in Kalyan station. He understood everything through gestures. 'I didn't know whether he was Hindu or Muslim. Who knows what compassion was in his heart, he took me to the canteen, and gave me tea. We slept together, in a gunny sack used to store sugar. I would go with him when he begged. I also got training in begging.'

'What kind of training did you get?' I ask.

'I was told that Arabs in the first class compartment give a lot. I would seek out the first class compartments and get money. I would say, "Give me 5 paise, 10 paise, I'm very hungry." They would give me 10-rupee notes.' He accompanied the mute everywhere. With the deaf-mute was another man, a deserter from the military. His fingers had all curled up from leprosy. He would also beg. People would tell Ramesh, 'Don't touch him, otherwise you'll also get the disease.' 'I didn't keep all these rules; I ate with him. He taught me swimming.

We would go swimming, off the Gateway of India. If we were late we would just sleep in VT station.'

When he got a big amount from begging he would buy treats for the other boys living on the station. One of those boys, Sadya, took Ramesh to his first movie theatre, and he saw an old film with Raj Kapoor. He was killing animals in the jungle. 'Then I started seeing films continuously. Even if I didn't have money for food I would beg and get money for movies.' The immersion in the Bombay movies had a fortunate side-effect for the Kannadiga: he started learning Hindi through them. 'I would see dishum-dishum pictures, and in story pictures I cried all the way.' In one of them he saw a woman that looked like his sister and he wept and wept.

The boy would find a place to sleep under the water fountain, or in a broken compartment, or in the guard's wagon of a freight train. One day he was crossing the tracks when he saw a big poster of the new Amitabh Bachchan movie. He stood and stared at the poster of Bachchan demolishing some villain on the poster, and so rapt was he that he did not hear the Deccan Queen bearing down on him fast. A coolie took a stick and hit him hard on the back with it, pushing him forward and out of the way just before the train got to the point he was standing at. After saving the boy's life, the coolie came to thrash him for his carelessness and Ramesh ran. 'The people on the station knew me.'

But as there were people who would save his life, there were also others who would kill him.

The boss of Kalyan station was a shopkeeper named Jahir Syed. He had a shop selling tea, cold drinks, and *sherbet*. 'Everything duplicate. Even the tea and sherbet had saccharine in it instead of sugar.' One day he shouted at Ramesh, 'Arre where are you from?' From the village, Ramesh replied. Syed put him to work for him, collecting water. One day Ramesh didn't fill the water tanks and Syed hit him. The boy cursed him. Syed asked his men to bring the boy back to him and hit him again and again in the stomach. Ramesh, enraged, picked up a rock and hit Syed on the collarbone, felling him to the ground. The deaf-mute told Ramesh that they should run away from the station, because Syed's boys would kill him. The deaf-mute knew people in Manmad, in the interior of Maharashtra. They hopped on a train going in that direction. When the ticket taker came through their compartment, they escaped him by standing on the coupling between the bogies. As the train neared Manmad, they needed to get off; if they got off at the station, they would be caught without a ticket and be thrown in jail. So the deaf-mute showed Ramesh the stairs next to the coupling leading to the top of the bogey, and how, if you climbed the ladder, you could turn a key on top of the coupling and the air would come out of the brakes and the train would slow down; and then you turned the key again and got off before the train resumed speed.

At Manmad the deaf-mute found work for Ramesh in a restaurant, and left the boy to go to Bhusaval. That same evening, as Ramesh was cleaning the tables, a patron cursed at him, 'Clean the tables properly!' Ramesh, angry at being cursed, threw a glass at him, and the management of the hotel beat him up and sat him to one side and told him they would call the police. So Ramesh ran away again, and kept running for some thirty kilometres, into the night. Running on the road, he came to a small village, where the dogs started barking. A man, coming out of his hut to piss, shouted into the darkness, 'Who is it?' Ramesh told him he was hungry and had come from Manmad, and the man took him into his home and gave him what the peasants eat: *bajri rotis* and *chutney*. He slept there, and in the morning, the man asked him if he would stay in the village and work. Ramesh said he had to go home, and walked out on the highway.

He hitched a ride with a truck going to Sholapur. For two days he had nothing to eat. He was drinking water at Sholapur station and felt dizzy and faint and fell down on the platform. A man revived him, but didn't give him anything to eat. He saw another man eating sugarcane and spitting out the shards. Ramesh went over and, as the man spat out the shards, gathered them from the floor and chewed and sucked on them. 'They were sweet.' Then, on a train passing by, he found better fare; some people who were eating rotis and *methi bhaji* gave him some of their food. He found a train going towards Bombay and, riding again on the coupling, got to Kalyan, still scared of Jahir Syed.

He lived on the station, always hiding from Syed, till one day the Sadibai – a policewoman from the children's remand home – caught him. She asked him where his parents were. 'I had no interest in my parents.' So she took him to the remand home in Bhiwandi. The remand room was a small jail crammed with over 200 boys from all over: Calcutta, Punjab, Madras. They were runaways and orphans, infested with lice; they were busy rubbing each others' bodies with the delousing medicine. For their bath, they were given just one jug of water each. Their meals consisted of two chapattis, a little dal, a little rice, tea and bread. The guards would make the boys sing religious songs, but Ramesh saw plenty of homosexual activity in the home, where he stayed for six months.

Meanwhile, someone had told the deaf-mute where Ramesh was, and he came to the remand home. He didn't have the money to get the boy out. So he made up a story; he came with a document saying that he was Ramesh's brother. Ramesh was released, and they walked all the way to Kalyan station from Bhiwandi; they didn't have money for the bus. At the station, they saw the father of Jahir Syed, the *dada*, selling pav-cake. The mute spoke to him, and he in turn instructed his son not to beat Ramesh. And he put Ramesh to work selling *batatawadas* on the trains. He did that for a while, until his friend Sadya recruited him into a better business: train-catching.

When the long-distance trains going all across the country out from Bombay pulled into Kalyan station, they would have one empty bogey for passengers without reservations who came aboard there. The scramble for seats would be desperate; getting a few inches of space on the seats could mean the difference between sitting or standing for several days and nights. So one of the group of train-catchers would get on at the previous station the train stopped at, Dadar, and hop into the Kalyan bogey. When the train pulled into

Kalyan the boy would wave his hand out of the empty compartment and the other train-catchers would run very fast along the arriving train, and jump on before it had come to a full stop. They had towels around their necks which they spread across the seats, claiming them. Then they sold the seats to the passengers for 10 or 20 rupees each. Often they would get into fights with passengers who challenged their claims on the seats. 'We beat up people.'

Ramesh had now been living on the station for two years. 'I became a big khiladi on Kalyan station, and got the knowledge of how to live.' The coolies would send him to fetch liquor. They would let him drink from it, too. By this time he was 16. 'We teased girls.' From Kalyan his friends would go to the whorehouses of Grant Road. 'My friends would say, what fun we had in Pilhaus. I was not much interested in sex, then or now. I only loved the movies. Sometimes English films would play at the theatres. I liked the action, the fights in the English films. The jumps, the flying, in air and water.'

With Jahir Bhai – the dada of the station who had threatened to kill him – Ramesh became such good friends that the dada wanted to take the boy with him to Delhi and convert him to Islam. He took him home to his family and fed him; 'that was my home when I wasn't on the platform.'

During his time at Kalyan Ramesh saw all life and death. One morning he was walking with his bottle of water to defecate by the tracks. As he squatted down, he saw a black thing. He looked closer; it was a human head. Its associated body was lying some distance away. He jumped backwards onto the platform and ran. The police came, and wouldn't touch the head; they made him pick it up. A man had written a suicide note, and then had laid himself across the tracks in front of the Calcutta Express.

On another day Ramesh and his friend Sadya were to catch seats on the 1:30 train. They bathed in the yard, under the big tap of the train water tank, and then Sadya went to his home to do his puja. When he came to the station, he told Ramesh about something that was worrying him: the garland he had decorated the god with had fallen by accident on his head, which had been freshly oiled. He took the garland off, and touched his hands to his head in the process – which was also a gesture asking forgiveness from the god – and the result was that Sadya had oily hands when he came to the station. His family had asked him not to go to work that day – they wanted him to come with them to Ulhasnagar – and Ramesh told him to clean off the oil, but Sadya wiped his hands on his clothes and said he would be all right.

Ramesh drank tea and ate wadas with him, and they saw the Nagpur Express coming in. 'I'll get the front, you get the back,' Ramesh said to him. They ran at great speed, and Ramesh grabbed the steel rail along the gate, and plunged into the bogey. He got in and spread himself across five seats and shouted for Sadya. He didn't see him, but he sold the seats and got down. He was walking near a juice stand when he saw a crowd of people bending down and looking under the train. A porter told Ramesh what had happened: As Sadya ran to grab the rails along the compartment that morning, his hands slipped on the steel, and he fell in between the running train and the platform. He was cut neatly in two pieces.

That day, Ramesh left train-catching. 'I got sadness in my heart.' He took up selling wadas again. One day he was in the Mahalaxmi Express and a group of boys bought four rupees worth of wadas from him. Then they shouted at him to fetch water. He shouted back that he wasn't in the business of selling water. They refused to pay, and he held one of the boys by the scruff of his neck and demanded his money. The boy looked at him, and said in astonishment, 'Hey, Ramesh!' It turned out that they were all from his village – Heerappa, Kundu, and others – and they had grown up herding animals together. They were going to the village, and said they had an extra ticket; he should come with them. He didn't go, but 'after they left the village started coming back to me.'

When the boys got to the village they told Ramesh's father that they'd seen his lost son on Kalyan station. In the six years that he'd been missing, his family had searched all over Bombay for him. On instructions from a pujari, they had taken water in a steel plate, then turned the water black and put a betel leaf in the water. Then the pujari asked them to look in the water, and they saw his face on the leaf. They asked Veerappa for a boon: if the god helped them find Ramesh, they would feed the whole town.

Immediately after the boys from the village spoke to him, Ramesh's father got on a train and came to Kalyan. He got to the station and was sitting in the canteen, whose owner was also from Karnataka. Just as the Ernakulam Express left, Ramesh sold his wadas and walked toward the canteen. 'I recognized my father at the canteen and was afraid. He saw me and got up and came toward me. I was very afraid, he would beat me, I should run. But he came running toward me and embraced me; he was sobbing. He was saying something in Kannada to me but I had forgotten the language. So he asked me in Hindi what happened. I replied that for fear of you I didn't go back to the village.'

His father took him back. As they approached the village, a crowd had gathered, from the three or four adjoining villages, to see this lost boy come back after six years. They were saying, 'Ramesha, Ramesha.' But he couldn't understand the rest of what they were saying. His sister, now married, came running to him and asked where he'd been all these years. She hugged him, crying. 'I felt very strange seeing the huge crowd in my home, but I couldn't understand and kept nodding.'

The person Ramesh wanted to see most was still in the fields: his mother. So he set out to look for her. Meanwhile his father had gone to the fields and told her, and she was running back to the village. As she ran, she still held a stick in her hand that she used to herd the animals. 'I saw my mother's face from far and I started crying a lot; I felt great sadness in my heart. My mother was saying all kinds of things in Kannada, she was clawing at my cheeks with love.' She took him home and said tenderly to her son, 'Uta marti?'

Ramesh looked around and asked, 'What is she saying?' A Hindi speaker translated: she was telling him to eat. He ate rice and vegetables. After everyone had left, his mother asked if he had brought any money back from the big city. He only had a 100 rupees in his pocket, and felt ashamed of himself. 'The other boys had earned 5000 rupees after staying in Bombay for one year. But this son, after staying away for seven years, had only brought a hundred rupees.' He had spent the money he earned in Bombay on his friends.

In the village, he started learning Kannada again. He herded animals. His father suggested work: in a government construction project, digging a canal. His sisters were already employed in the project. There was a line of five women along the 40 feet to the bottom of the canal. A basket of earth would be passed up all the way along the line to Ramesh, at the top, who would throw the earth over the side. It was very hard work. The sun beat on his head, and he sweated a lot. He worked eight hours a day, and made a total of six rupees a day; the women earned four rupees. In Bombay, he had made up to 200 rupees a day in the train-catching. 'I realized now that life was very hard in the village.' He worked for three months on the canal. He was 18 by this time; he said to his mother that he didn't like it there, he would go back to Bombay and this time, he would save money. He tried two or three times to run away to Bombay, would go as far as Asikeri, but would then feel bad about abandoning his mother and sisters, and would turn back.

'I remembered Bombay: my friends, the movies, my fun in Bombay. Nobody to tell me anything, ekdum bindaas. The trains, the cars, the buses.' His village friends would take him to see Kannada movies, which bored him. 'The heroes had no style. The scenes were totally third class, like stage plays.' His father, meanwhile, would go to other people's houses to recite the Harikatha. He knew all the stories, of the old kings and gods. But Ramesh didn't like this. 'One day I shouted at him; I don't like your shouting in other people's houses, they will think you are a servant. Another guru explained that I shouldn't say such things, god won't like it.' It was clear that Ramesh had become a total misfit in the village, and he left for Bombay again, two years after he'd come back.

At Kalyan station all his friends came on to the train and gave him free wadas and cold drinks. They said he looked very good in his clothes, not like a *tapori*. His uncle at Walshingham was unwilling to put him up again. 'He was in Kalyan station for such a long time, we can't trust him.' Then Ramesh's brother put him to work in a tea canteen at Nana Chowk, washing glasses. He hated the dirty work, and felt like going back to Kalyan station, 'but I remembered my mother, and thought I might get crushed under the train.' After four months he found better work in the parcel office. The man running the office was a Shetty from Kannada, and he hired his countryman. It was good work – it shut at five, and Ramesh had Saturdays and Sundays off.

But there was trouble in the village. His sister had married their uncle's son, to save money on the dowry. Shortly after the wedding, she came home to her parents' and wept in front of all their photographs; her husband's heart was not with her. He loved another. One morning she left at six in the morning with the manure to the fields, in the mist. The villagers were wondering why she was going so early, why she was so sad. 'When people in the village saw my sister, normally, they were very happy.' She spread the manure in the fields, and then she went up to a well and put her feet in it. A villager, defecating nearby, saw her, and then saw her disappear into the well, but he didn't go up to her because he thought she was bathing, and as a man, he shouldn't approach her alone. But when he didn't see her emerge from the well, he ran to the village and raised an alarm. 'They came to the well and saw her standing like this, with her hands above her head, in the well with water just above her head.'

His sister had enjoyed great respect in the village; they were all howling now with grief. Along with his mother, they went off in search of her husband, who was hiding in his lover's house. They broke the house down and dragged him out, thrashing him. He was crying that he didn't know why she would do this. Ramesh's uncles went at him with bamboo sticks and would have killed him, 'but some educated people saved him.' His mother wrote to Ramesh and he went back. 'We didn't inform the police; we have a custom that if anyone commits suicide we don't tell the police, we gather and close ranks.'

After he returned to Bombay, he got his brother's old job at Sagar Kunj, right next to Dariya Mahal, working as a domestic. 'I had never seen such a flat in my life. The TV, the A/C, the tiles, the fan, the color. My brother told me, 'Don't touch anything here, don't steal.' I had to do the clothes, the dusting, the washing... good work.' Once he was at his uncle's garage, sitting at the wheel of his uncle's Ambassador car. His uncle shouted at him to get out of the car. Ramesh felt hurt, and asked his employer's wife for money to learn driving. He went to the Goodluck Driving School and in 15 days he had learned the basics of driving. Then, while washing his employer's car, he would sometimes take it out for a spin. During one such joyride he got into a fender-bender, and pushed it all the way back to Sagar Kunj and told the employer that someone had banged it in the parking lot. But the employer found out the truth, and said he would take Ramesh to the police. He left that job, but he had his licence.

His uncles found out that he could drive. 'They started respecting me.' He found another job as a domestic, earning a thousand a month from the owner, Vachmani. Along with his brother, Ramesh was able to marry off his surviving sister for one lakh rupees in Shimoga, including 30,000 for the dowry. The money was raised from the informal banking network that many migrants in Bombay use, the 'pund' or 'BC'. He explains the system: a group of 30 people deposit a thousand rupees a month into the pund. Whenever someone has an urgent need for money, they bid for it, saying they will take thirty thousand minus one thousand, minus two thousand, minus ten thousand. Those who lift the money early get that amount cut from the payout. But those who can wait till the end of the cycle get the full thirty thousand.

Meanwhile, he was still practising his driving in the owner's car. Once he banged it, and Vachmani was fine with it, but his wife said something insulting and Ramesh left their employ. The next job he had was with a jeweller who treated him like family. When they drove to Nashik he ate with them, in good restaurants, rather than being given a few rupees to eat at some truckstop. 'I found out what a boy in a big family enjoys. I found all the happiness that I didn't find in Kalyan.' When they went to Varanasi for a pilgrimage they took along as their driver – in a plane. It was, of course, the first time for Ramesh. 'My ears burst; they gave me cotton.' In the three years he stayed with the jeweller, 'I saw what a big man in the world enjoys. The tension he has: of business. A big man can't become small. A poor man can live without bread, such people can't. Their children can't live poorly. When business is down they still has to maintain their lifestyle. They can't sleep well. they sleep four hours a night, then wake up early and think, 'I have to make money, increase my business.'

When his brother was to get married, Ramesh again went back to the village. With a friend, he had to go to a house in a nearby village to give the invitation for the wedding, and there was a girl sitting in the room, alone, and they talked. He liked the way she was talking; he thought she was smart. She brought him a glass of milk to drink. His friend was kidding him, telling him that she was so nice. Then her mother came into the room. Ramesh looked up at the lady, and told her, 'I want to marry your daughter.'

Her mother laughed. 'Whose son are you?'

The girl, who was only 16, got shy and ran away. Later, she told Ramesh that she had liked him on first sight, too; 'I had eaten a lot at the jeweller's house and looked like a man from high society.' He was 25.

He went back home and told his father that he'd met the girl he wanted to marry. They had an argument; the girls' family couldn't give much dowry. They had themselves given a lot of dowry for Ramesh's sister's wedding, and his father was counting on the dowry for Ramesh to come in and right the economics. 'Then we had a fight. I was obstinate; I went the very next day and got engaged to the girl.'

Eight days after his engagement – nine days after he had first set eyes on her – he got married. (He says, 'I got married,' as opposed to 'we got married.') But even during the brief period of his engagement, he had other offers. His sisters' husband's sisters liked him a lot – they thought he looked like Ravichandra or Kamalahasan, film heroes of the South. They told him so.

Ramesh and his brother came back to Bombay with their new brides and installed them in a room in Worli that a garage mechanic rented out to them for 300 a month. When Ramesh went back to the jeweller's family, he found that the substitute driver had replaced him. So he found work with a Jain diamond merchant. But he didn't get along with an old Maharashtrian maid in the house. Her sons were involved in all sorts of criminal activities. After a while, Ramesh left the job. Eight days after he left, the merchant was kidnapped at gunpoint from his car. He was robbed and let go.

In the police inquiry, they asked the merchant about his servants. He said that he had one who hadn't come for a few days. The police arrested the robbers, and one of them said he knew someone named Ramesh. Three police jeeps pulled up outside Ramesh's house in Worli. By this time, he was driving a taxi, and had just come home with a headache from his long day. His brother had been arrested and released, but they now took Ramesh to the police station. They asked him if he knew the robbers; he said he didn't. Meanwhile, he saw how the police were torturing one of the robbers: 'They had him up on the table, and had tied his feet together, and were beating the soles of his feet. Then they would have him get up on the table, and tell him to jump, and then hit him on the buttocks with their sticks.'

Ramesh was spared the beating, since the robber said he didn't know him, he was the wrong Ramesh. But they kept him jailed overnight anyway. In the morning his employer came to the station, and the police released Ramesh. He had to keep coming to the station for the next few days. He confronted his employer's wife. 'I said, how could you do this, I haven't even touched any valuable in your house. I choked up and wept there.'

One day, driving his taxi, he got talking to the passenger. The passenger said he had been adopted by the madam of a whorehouse, and now had started his own brothel. He needed a driver to take his girls to their customers in the hotels, and that was how Ramesh started working for him. He took the girls to good hotels and not so good ones, from the Mansara Hotel in Bandra to the President in Cuffe Parade. He got paid 5,000 a month; there were 35 girls. Most of them were from Andhra Pradesh, Nepal, and Calcutta, and the odd one from Delhi. The house was located near the Dreamland Theater. He got to know the girls' stories. One girl was in college. She had been in love with a boy, 'who used her and abandoned her.' A girlfriend had brought her, broken-hearted, to Bombay and this line. Another was only 13, and from Andhra. When the police raided the house she was hidden away. 'I talked to her. She was supporting her family.'

Another kind of migrant labour, the same as his own. But the girls did not cry in his car, and they seemed happy to him. When a nervous customer would ask him, 'the girl will cooperate, won't she?' he would respond, 'I'm not a pimp, you seduce her yourself.' One evening the police were about to raid a hotel he had brought six girls to; the party would select two or three from them. The watchman warned Ramesh and he took his bevy of girls and parked by a lake. The police came up and tapped the window, and asked him what he was doing. He said he was taking the girls home from a disco, and they let him go. 'I dropped them home and left the job.'

I ask Ramesh if he partook of the girls. He did not. He also abstained from sex in his next job, which was as a truckdriver. A relative of his who lived in Dombivili owned five trucks. Ramesh began as a second driver, a double, for three months. 'I would empty the goods in Thane – chemicals, acid so strong that it will burn your hands if it falls on you – and supply it to the textile factories around there. Then I would head back to Madras to get the material. It took three days. I had great fun driving a truck. I drank. The truck ran tanatan and I was high. I drank anything – country, anything. Other drivers had ganja and drove.' They needed the drink and the drugs for strength to drive their long shifts, which could be more than 24 hours at a stretch.

They also needed women. Truck-drivers consider sexual encounters on the highway part of daily life; often, a driver will have an erection first, then look by the side of the road to look for a woman carrying a telltale object such as a blanket. If he finds one, he stops the truck, negotiates with the woman, gets on top of her and inserts his penis, ejaculates, and gets up and back into his truck in under five minutes. When Ramesh would stop at a dhaba to eat, the girls from the surrounding villages would come to do their business, sell jasmine necklaces to hang up in the truck, and fall into the truckdrivers' arms. 'I didn't do anything.' They would tease him: 'Don't you have anything in you?' But Ramesh was afraid. 'Once I just touched one and I broke out in warts, and then I was very afraid.'

'The truckdrivers just do it in the jungle. They spread a sheet and do it. I let my conductor do anything; I let him enjoy. But I got very disgusted when he did it and climbed back in the truck. Throw a bucket over yourself and then get in, I told him.'

He drove the truck for a year and a half. One night he was making the eight-hour drive from Bangalore to Mangalore with a load of tomatoes. As the truck left Bangalore, it ran over a serpent on the road. 'I heard the sound under the wheel – khach, khach.' It was a bad portent. He drove along, picked up four passengers for a hundred rupees, dropped them off in Hasan. He started feeling sleepy. At the next town he splashed his face with water, but the water smelt of fish. Coming down from the ghats, he picked up a new bride and groom going to the temple, and dropped them off.

Then, just before a bridge, he lost control of the wheel, and the truck went down the hill, breaking a light pole, and plunged 50 feet down a ravine. People from a passing bus pulled him out. He was only bruised, but was kept in the hospital for five days. His employer drove him to his village. He got out of the car and was walking home in the rain through the fields, when he heard the sound of wailing. When he walked into his room he found the women of his household crying, lamenting his death. Upon seeing him, they were astonished, and they said to his wife, 'Look, your man is alive.' She made him give up the lorry.

At this point he decided to try his luck outside India. He sold his wife's jewels and raised 30,000 rupees and went to an agent to find employment in Saudi Arabia. The agent kept Ramesh waiting for a fortnight and then gave him a driving test. Ramesh gave him all his money, and the agent said he would be able to go the very next day. Elated, Ramesh got a passport, and gave it to the agent.

He was asked to come to the airport at 5:30 am the following morning; the agent would be there with his tickets and passport and visa. Ramesh got there, ready to board his flight to his bright future, and waited for the agent. He waited till 5:30 pm. He was waiting outside the airport, where there were hordes of people. 'I ran up and down the airport; I checked all the taxis coming in. I tried to remember his face. I phoned my brother-in-law to check for him in his office. There was no office, and he wasn't in his hotel room.'

Then he found out that the agent had decamped with the passports and money of Ramesh and three other suckers like him. 'Then I felt suicidal. What had I done?' Not only had he sold his wife's jewellry, he had borrowed another fifteen thousand. He kept looking for the agent, all over the city, for another eight days. One day he was looking for him in Sion station when he saw a man selling medicine to exterminate fleas. 'I asked him, "If a man drinks this, will he die?" He said, "Immediately".' Ramesh bought a bottle for 15 rupees and went home. There was trouble at home; his wife was sore at him for losing the money, and got irritated at him for minor matters. 'Then a friend, seeing me in tension, said, "Why this tension? Let's drink rum".'

As they were drinking at the bar, Ramesh asked his friend, 'If a man drinks poison after drinking alcohol, will it affect him?' His friend replied, 'It will increase the potency.' So Ramesh drank a quarter bottle of rum and went home and woke up his wife in the middle of the night. He said, 'Look, Sudha, what do you feel, I have lost money?' In answer, she told him to go away and not come to her bed. Whereupon he gave her two slaps. Her sister woke up and began yelling at Ramesh. In the midst of the altercation, Ramesh opened the bottle of flea poison and upended it over his mouth. 'As soon as it touched my lips everything in my stomach, the rum, everything, came out and the whole house was filled with a stink.' His wife's sister gave her two more slaps: 'Aren't you seeing what he's drinking?' He fell unconscious and woke up in the hospital. 'I was shamed, how could I be alive?' But his family all comforted him, 'So what if you've lost money, you'll earn some more.' His friends came around and told him that it was a sin to kill himself. His wife wept.

He took his wife to the village and left her there, and came back to Dariya Mahal and started driving a taxi.

One of his regular customers in the taxi was a Parsi businessman, and Ramesh told him his story, how he'd lost the money and been duped by the agent. The Parsi had a relative who owned a company in Dubai; he promised to send Ramesh there. Ramesh got another passport made, and worked at the Parsi's house for a fortnight. He learnt cooking. And he gave his savings – 10,000 rupees – to the Parsi for the plane ticket to Dubai. 'They said there is great leisure there.' He finally made it to the Gulf, in 1996, and went to the house of his employer, a bad tempered man named Poonawala, where he was told he would work as a cook.

He was a cook all right – for the dogs. Part of his duties involved making *keema* for the owners' dogs, after bathing them. He had gone from being an assistant beggar to working as a cook for a dog. This was not the life he had imagined for himself in fabulous Dubai.

For three months he woke at six in the morning, cleaned the house, watered the garden, sent the kids to school and took care of the dogs. He was not driving, he was only doing housework. When he remonstrated with his employers they sent him to work in their factory, where he had to work 14 hours a day. It was very hot there and there was no A/C. The factory made plastic cups for Emirates flights. Ramesh worked at a huge grinder that ground plastic waste into powder. He was constantly afraid that he would get caught in the grinder. But the money was better than he'd been getting in Poonawala's house, which was 500 a month in 'Dubai currency'; he got a 1000 to work in the factory. But he had to eat in the canteen, Malabari food, and got sick. He told his employers that he was a driver, not like the other Malabaris. He said he wanted to go back to India. They said he couldn't. So then he offered to work again at their home, which several previous servants had left after being ill-treated. He was abused for transgressions such as sleeping in the air-conditioned room after a day's work.

Meanwhile, one of the people from his village had also come to Dubai, and told Ramesh that his wife was seriously ill; she had his second child in her stomach. Around this time, a gold chain disappeared from the house and all the servants were lined up by the police and interrogated. Unlike Bombay, they weren't beaten, but Ramesh still felt very bad. He told his employers that his wife was serious. They replied that they had found out that his wife had actually had an abortion. He argued with them, and they made out a return ticket for him. 'I prayed to God that day, "thank you God".' Then he opened his bags in front of his employer and said, 'Look, check, and check me too.' They gave him a 1000 of their currency, and he left for India. As soon as he woke up the next day, he went to Narayan Dabholkar Road to the people who had sent him to Dubai. He left his passport and return ticket in their care. Then he left for the village and found that his employers had lied; his wife had not had an abortion; the baby was in her stomach. It was a daughter, like the first child. He had wanted to be sterilized right after the first girl, but everyone told him to wait, he might have a son next time. A year later came the second daughter. 'Then I was afraid that if I had a third she would also be a daughter. My wife said, "your work is not so good, better you have an operation".' And so he did; there won't be any more children.

He stayed in the village for a year and a half, driving a bus. When he went back to Bombay he asked for his passport back and the people he'd given it to said they didn't have it. Ramesh went to the Malabar Hill police station and told them what happened. The police asked him to file a complaint, 'but I said they are big people and I am small and I won't stand any chance against them.' His wife told him to forget it, why did he want to go abroad anyway.

Despite all his troubles, he liked what he saw in Dubai. He remembers that his employers took him to a Hindi movie there, *Rangeela*. If he had found driving work there he would have stayed for 10, 15 years. 'It is clean there, not crowded. There are no wastrels there, everyone is doing their work. I liked that system. It is much better than Bombay; it is clean, there is no business on the sidewalks, no slums. Each office has an A/C. The poor there are not as poor as Indians.'

He started driving a taxi again in Bombay. A *sheth* from Muscat asked him to come to the Gulf again but he had lost interest. When he is not driving the taxi he does other kinds of work. He has worked as a bootlegger. 'In Borivili they make country liquor. They keep it in tire tubes. They mix the pure alcohol with some chemicals and water and measure the degree of alcohol. Some mix tobacco, some mix cardamom essence, so it will be scented with cardamom. I have to bring six or seven of the tubes and drive at great speed to the liquor dens, to Tardeo, Nana Chowk, Khetwadi, and throw out the tubes. I bring the stuff in the evenings. Sometimes I am checked, but there is a setting.'

'Since then I have been driving a taxi in Dariya Mahal. My wife lives in Nalasopara and I have two kids. I drive the taxi and I go home. Thus my life has passed.'

Ramesh has often tried to look for the deaf-mute who had taken him in at the station. But he has disappeared. Ramesh wants to take him back to his village and take care of him in his old age. Jahir Bhai, the dada, has a flourishing business on the station. Of the other boys with him who lived on the platform, one became a rickshaw driver, one is a tea vendor, another a tailor. One boy named Krishna, a train catcher, lost a leg in his work. Another train catcher, who was blind in one eye, slipped from a running train after catching it, and fell in between the tracks, and lost his arm as well.

He sometimes meets runaways like himself. Once he met a Kannadiga boy at Majestic bus stand who was begging. He asked him in Kannada, 'Why are you begging?' The boy replied, 'I don't have enough to eat.' Ramesh gave him 20 rupees, to eat, and told him to buy soap, have a bath, and go to any eatery and ask for work. 'I meet many such boys and I give them some money and I talk to them, "Don't beg, work, don't let me see you here again." I think, I too have seen such days myself.'

In Bombay, says Ramesh, 'even if a man is selling bananas, his expenses are met and he can send some money home. In Bombay, even if a man sells stones, ornamental stones, on the road, he can have an income. There is no other city in India like Bombay, no other city where you can earn so much. In Bombay nobody will ask you: "Where are you from, why are you here?" You can die, sleep, breed on the road and no one will ask you.'

It is the most hospitable city. Come, and bring your family also. But things are changing; the city's hospitality is being abused. Ramesh remembers a time when everybody could work and live happily in Bombay. Now, he thinks, people don't want to work; they just want money without work.

Ramesh was in Dariya Mahal on the ground when I was there in the air, on the ninth floor. He has been living in the Dariya Mahal *chawls* since 1982, and has watched its decline. 'First Dariya Mahal was known as the place where big people stayed. Now Dariya Mahal has no value, its show is spoilt, because of the underground garages. There is no control over who is coming or going. People go to bathroom on the seaside and bathe in the gutter water. From the flats you can see them shitting. In the underground the stench is so strong you will want to run out.'

There are upwards of a thousand people living in those garages, he says, Biharis and *bhaiyyas* mostly, 'and it is all rotten.' The lower row of garages have not a single car in them; the residents are related to the liftmen and watchmen of the three buildings, or complete outsiders. They boast: 'I have a bungalow on Nepean Sea Road.' They cannot be removed, even though the structure is collapsing. The watchmen of the buildings are also bhaiyyas, and so they don't bother the garage-dwellers. There was a *lafda* there when Ramesh was in the village, someone was badly hurt. 'Three-fourths of Bombay is now people from UP-Bihar. I know them, since most of the taxi-drivers are such people, and only ten per cent of them are good.'

He doesn't have much respect for those who claim to be the 'sons of the soil' either. 'The Maharashtrians are not hard workers. They just have two days' dreams. They fill their bellies today, and don't think about tomorrow.' Bal Thackeray had boasted that he would turn Bombay into Singapore, 'but he has made it into UP. In a little while you'll see cycle rickshaws here.'

The city's contrasts amaze him. 'There are people who don't have money to eat tomorrow. There are also people who have so much money they don't even know how much they have. The people who don't have money are thinking, I should do some crooked business and become like them. They can't become like them from hard work, or a job. The people who have hereditary wealth – money making money – will stay like that. The small people spend all the money they make. They don't save it for the next generation. Who becomes big? The people who do goondagiri, netagiri. They who become corporators, and then leaders. Now there is a bhai in each house.'

He had recently shifted from Dariya Mahal to Nalasopara, site of the birth of a two-headed baby who was considered a goddess. His wife had gone to see the baby, but by then there wasn't much of a crowd around the goddess. There had been another case in Kerala 16 years ago, the crowd had learnt, of a baby with two heads, who had grown up and joined a circus. The event had been robbed of its singularity.

If business is good Ramesh makes 200 a day driving his taxi; if not he makes a hundred. He averages four to five thousand a month.

In Nalasopara he pays 550 a month for a room and a kitchen. The older daughter, four years old, is in an English-medium school. Her fees is 500 rupees a month. 'She speaks abcd well.'

His family has now been in Bombay with him for eight months, 'but I have now enjoyed family and want to put them back in the village.' He puts the taxi back in his uncle's garage in Dariya Mahal at nine in the evening, then takes the train to Nalasopara and reaches there at midnight, then bathes and eats and sleeps by one. Then he has to wake up at 4:30 and take the 5:30 train. All of Sunday he sleeps. Once a month he takes his daughters to a temple or to the seaside at Chowpatty. 'My girls are not interested in me. Only in their mother, because I don't see them at all.'

Poor as he was on Kalyan station, he had no tension. 'Now that I have two children and a wife there is a lot of tension. Now I don't like Bombay, I don't like the crowds, and I think about going to the village.' His family now has fields, 50 coconut trees, and a borewell in the village. When he goes to his village he does the *jatra*, walking on live coals, with the god supported on his head. He shows me the scarred soles of his feet.

He speaks about what he wants from the fates. 'I want to get my two girls married off into good houses. I want to save a little money, put some money in my daughters' names, and live my life with my wife.'